Learning to
TRUST
IN THE LORD

Learning to TRUST IN THE LORD

Michelle L. Martin

Second edition. First printed in 2008.

Copyright © 2017 by Michelle L. Martin
www.MichelleLMartin.com

All rights reserved. No part of this publication may be reproduced, distributed, or transmitted in any form or by any means, including photocopying, recording, or other electronic or mechanical methods, without the prior written permission of the author, except in the case of brief quotations embodied in critical reviews and certain other noncommercial uses permitted by copyright law.

Editing: Brittney Okada Perkins
Design: Angie Lawrence

ISBN:
ebook 9781630729196
paperback 9781630729202

Library of Congress Control Number: 2017932698

Izzard Ink Publishing Company
PO Box 522251
Salt Lake City, Utah 84152
www.izzardink.com

ACKNOWLEDGMENTS

Special thanks to my angel parents for watching over me and this project!

Thanks to the following for helping make this book a reality: Shane and Heather Lyon, Amy Olsen, Cecy Burtenshaw, Sarah DeLange, Heather Elwell, and Brittney Okada Perkins.

A special thank you to Angie Lawrence for the design work.

Last but not least, I express appreciation to all my family members and friends for their continued support and love!

This book is dedicated to my nieces and nephews Marissa, Aaron, Sara, Angela, Keaton, Emily, Brandon, and Brooklyn.

Also, to my siblings, Mattye and Malcolm.

CONTENTS

Introduction ix

Chapter 1: Put Your Scuba Gear Down! 1

Chapter 2: Choices 8

Chapter 3: Following the Counsel of Our Leaders 18

Chapter 4: When the Spirit Speaks, Don't Delay 27

Chapter 5: Stand Still in the Furnace of Affliction 40

Chapter 6: It's Never Too Late to Pray 47

Chapter 7: Learning to Laugh at Yourself 61

Chapter 8: Remembering Life's Little Miracles 67

Chapter 9: God Bless America 77

Chapter 10: Women Who Have Gone Before Us 82

Chapter 11: Trust in the Lord 94

INTRODUCTION

My life experiences have taught me that the choices we make can show Heavenly Father that we trust Him, and that we should recognize the little miracles in our daily lives. The Lord is aware of us—aware of our hopes and dreams. Above all, I've learned that we can trust Him.

When going through excruciating challenges, it can be hard to trust the Lord and to lay our will at His feet. I believe this is one of our greatest challenges in life. In his last address, Elder Neal A. Maxwell said in April 2004 General Conference: "As you submit your wills to God, you are giving Him the only thing you can actually give Him that is really yours to give. Don't wait too long to find the altar or to begin to place the gift of your wills upon it! No need to wait for a receipt; the Lord has His own special ways of acknowledging. He not only knows the names of all the stars (see Psalms 147:4; Isaiah 40:26); He knows your names and all your heartaches and your joys!"[1]

Trusting the Lord is the only way to true happiness. As you learn of Him, you will gain knowledge that He truly is all-powerful and all-loving. Staying close to Him and saturating yourself with His Spirit will empower you to trust in Him and in His perfect timing for you.

This book includes stories and ideas to help you learn to place your confidence in the Lord. At the end of each chapter, you will find an action—a specific way to apply a certain principle in your life. I hope this book inspires you to know that God lives and that He loves you.

Throughout the book, there will be challenges, so be prepared to work while you read. I encourage you to write in your journal as thoughts come to your mind. President Henry B. Eyring understood the importance of keeping a journal:

> "I would ponder this question: 'Have I seen the hand of God reaching out to touch us or our children or our family today?' As I kept at it, something began to happen. As I would cast my mind over the day, I would see evidence of what God had done for one of us that I had not recognized in the busy moments of the day.
>
> As that happened, and it happened often, I realized that trying to remember had allowed God to show me what He had done. More than gratitude began to grow in my heart. Testimony grew. I became ever more certain that our Heavenly Father hears and answers prayers. I felt more gratitude for the softening and refining that come because of the Atonement of the Savior Jesus Christ. And I grew more confident that the Holy Ghost can bring all things to our remembrance—even things we did not notice or pay attention to when they happened."[2]

If you keep a journal as you go through this process of pondering, it may change your life and help you to see your own miracles.

Chapter 1

PUT YOUR SCUBA GEAR DOWN!

One of my favorite stories in the *Bible* is the Lord's deliverance of the children of Israel from the Egyptians. Through the prophet Moses, the Lord showed His power by bringing terrible plagues upon the Egyptians; from painful boils to infestations of frogs, flies, and locusts, to dreadful storms and water turned into blood, and to ultimately the death of all firstborn of the Egyptians, including Pharaoh's son. Finally, Pharaoh told the Israelites to depart, and they did so rejoicing. Shortly after leaving Egypt, the Israelites arrived on the shores of the Red Sea, and when they saw Pharoah's soldiers coming, they murmured, already forgetting the miraculous power of their Deliverer. "For," they said, "it had been better for us to serve the Egyptians, than that we should die in the wilderness" (Exodus 14:12). But didn't the Lord just perform multiple miracles in order to free His children from bondage? How could they forget so easily?

I believe this story relates to us today because like you I have faced my own Red Seas. Through these times, I've learned that the Lord always knows what is best for us. And somehow, some way, He always parts our Red Seas. But sometimes when I jump right in and start to walk on dry ground, I walk a few feet, look up, and see the big walls of water, only to then yank on my backpack to check to see if my scuba gear is still in there "just in case." Just in case He lets the walls of water fall on me, or just in case He leaves me on my own, I guess. And when I have those unrealistic fears, I've felt like the Lord is asking, "Michelle, don't you remember the other miracles—the frogs, the flies, and the locust?" And then I can imagine Him saying, "Michelle, you put that scuba gear down! Move forward with faith!"

We have been taught to be prepared in all things. But when the Lord says to trust Him, He is bound to His promise when we do (D&C 82:10).

Before sharing a Red Sea from my past, I'll need to give a bit of background. As I grew up, my family was not affiliated with any religion, but my mother taught me faith and courage in so many ways. When I was 17 years old, I was introduced to the The Church of Jesus Christ of Latter-Day Saints by a friend from high school. That time of my life was particularly difficult, as my parents had separated, and like most teenagers, I was trying to find out who I was. I was also searching for religious truth and pondering questions like: Why am I here? Where am I going? What is my purpose in life? Is there a God and does He know me? I considered taking the missionary discussions. During that time, my mother went to a local LDS bookstore and purchased a book called *A Marvelous Work and Wonder* by LeGrand Richards. My mother said to me, "I might not be able to answer some of your questions about life, but maybe this book will help you." So I read that inspiring book and found the answers to my questions. My mother as well as my sister and my LDS friends encouraged me to continue meeting with the missionaries, and I was baptized a few weeks later.

Though my mother never joined an organized religion, she certainly helped me find the answers to life's important questions. She urged me to grow in faith, although she didn't have the full truth of the gospel herself. Looking back, I realize just how much my mother loved me.

A few years later when I was preparing to leave for a church mission, my mother asked if she could speak at my missionary farewell. She knew it was a custom in the Church for the missionary's parents to speak. Again, she taught me a lesson of faith and courage. If I weren't a member of the Church, I would have felt very intimidated to speak in front of one of their congregations. She did speak at my farewell, and she articulated her thoughts well as she spoke of her love for me and her belief in what I was doing.

Before I left to go to the Missionary Training Center in Provo, Utah, my mother and I agreed to write every week during my mission. She never missed a week. She also met with my bishop to arrange the money donations she would give each month to help support my mission.

Two months into my mission, my mother was diagnosed with terminal ovarian cancer, and initially her doctors said she would only live another four to six months. This was a hard time for me, and I felt as though the Red Sea was in front of me and there was no way to cross it. I pleaded with the Lord to help me to know what to do, especially since my sister and I were the only members of the Church in our family. How would my family react if I were to stay on my mission while my mother was dying at home? After much prayer, the answer from the Lord came with perfect clarity: I was to stay and complete my mission. I knew Heavenly Father would take care of my mother and that He would take care of me.

My next dilemma was how to tell my mother my decision, and to convince her that this was what I should do. A few days after I found out she had cancer, on Christmas Day, my mother and I spoke on the telephone. Before I could say anything about staying on my mission, my mother told me that she thought I should stay! Her exact words were, "As long as you are doing God's special work, I know I'll be taken care of." What a miracle this was for me! My mother had so much faith and courage.

Knowing that my mission rules only allowed communication through letters and limited telephone calls, my mother had written to my mission president asking him to tell me she had cancer. Here is a portion of my mother's letter:

> "Happy Holidays to you and all the wonderful young adults you are working with. I'm so proud of Michelle; she is a shining star in my eyes. I write you in hopes I'm doing the right thing by asking to please explain and tell Michelle I'll be having surgery next week after Christmas. I had my back drained of fluid, which had build up around my lungs—this she knows. She doesn't know anything else. After many

tests the doctors have discovered I have cancer. They are unable to tell how far it has spread. I'll have surgery and chemotherapy treatments, with all good faith I hope to return to work by the end of January. I do not want Michelle to come home; I would just like her to continue work there and I would like her prayers.

After discussing this with her sister, she thought I should write to you. I'm sorry to leave such a burden on your shoulders, but I will be fine, and I truly would prefer her to continue her missionary work. I believe I'll gain her strength through her work and God's special love."

The next week, I remember looking in the yellow pages during personal scripture study. I thought I would check with the airlines about flights, just in case I should go home. While thumbing through the pages I was kindly reminded of Heavenly Father's tender answer for me to stay. I felt like He was saying to me, "Michelle, put your scuba gear down—you don't need it. Trust me. Remember your past miracles of the frogs, the lice, the flies, and the locust in your life" (Exodus 6–14).

At that time I chose to stay on my mission. On two different occasions, my mother was taken to the intensive care unit (ICU), and both times the doctors weren't sure if she would make it through the night. These made for particularly hard days, but each time she was in ICU, I knew I was to continue on my mission. My mother even went through a period of remission for about three months. When the doctors discovered that the cancer had reappeared, they said it had come back with a vengeance and that she had less than a month to live. It was a very hard decision, but I ended up coming home from my mission several weeks early. When I first saw my mother, she asked what was going to happen to her when she died. At first, I wasn't prepared to hear this from the person who had always been so strong for me. I loved her so much, and this was hard to face. Everything was changing so quickly that my life felt like an emotional roller coaster.

One night when my mother was very ill due to the chemotherapy, the nurses put her on oxygen. She also had multiple IVs in her arm. She and I both knew that her time to pass was soon. So I sat by her hospital bedside and said, "Mom, I am now going to teach you about the plan of salvation and why we are here and where you are going to go." I told her that this was what I had been teaching on my mission in Illinois for the last 16 months. I asked her how she felt about this, and she said she was ready to hear it. For the next few hours and with the power of the Holy Ghost, I taught the woman I loved more than anyone else in the world about God's miraculous plan and the spirit world. She was so filled with the Spirit that I knew she knew that it was true, and I could actually see peace come across her face. A few days later—one week after I came home from my mission—she slipped into a coma. A week after that, she passed away peacefully.

I'm so grateful for my mother's amazing example of faith, courage, and selflessness. Although this was such a difficult time in my life, looking back, I can clearly see the Lord's hand guiding me all the way. While there were moments when I felt like I was standing in a narrow crevice, barely able to keep my balance as if the walls of water from my own Red Sea were about to close in on me, they did not. The Lord kept his promise to never forsake me (Deuteronomy 4:31).

CHALLENGE

Write down in your journal (if you don't have one, get one) your past Red Seas—your obstacles and challenges in life. Then make a list of past miracles (your own frogs, lice, flies, and locust), and how Heavenly Father helped you cross your Red Seas. It could be anything: the miracle of good weather for a special event, an acceptance letter for college, the birth of a child, the timing of the death of a loved one, or an unexpected financial blessing. It won't take you long to start realizing the daily miracles in your life.

Chapter 2

CHOICES

The summer between my junior and senior years in high school, my dear friend Lisa experienced a terrible tragedy in her family. Her father, a psychiatrist, was shot and killed in his office by one of his male patients. Understandably, this was an extremely difficult time for Lisa and her family.

A few years after high school, Lisa mentioned that she needed to forgive her father's murderer so that she could move forward in life. Lisa later became a nurse and understood more about mental illness and what her father had dedicated his life to doing; helping the mentally ill to become functioning members of society. He helped thousands.

Lisa never had complete closure with her father's death, so it has been important for her to keep the lines of communication open with her husband, children, and other family members and friends. She doesn't like to leave anything unresolved, even just overnight, and she never wants to live with the regret of having unfinished words to a loved one. Lisa possesses a healthy sense of self and has triumphed over a terrible tragedy.

When I spoke with her recently, she said that hating her father's murderer or holding a grudge against him was a waste of energy. She explained that it was a choice to forgive and to not hold a grudge. Obviously, such understanding didn't come to Lisa overnight—the deepest insights never do. But I am grateful for her powerful example. In the face of adversity, Lisa chose to move forward and focus on the good things in her life.

One of the greatest gifts we have been given here on earth is the gift of agency. Elder Richard G. Scott explained, "The right of moral agency is so important to our Father in Heaven that he was willing to loose one-third of his spirit children so that it would be preserved. You can make the decisions you choose to make. But you cannot choose the consequences. They are determined by divine law. Should your choices be wrong, there is a path back through repentance. When the conditions of repentance are fully met, the Atonement of the Savior provides a release from the demands of justice for the errors made."[3]

Every day of our lives, we make choices—big ones that affect the rest of our lives and small ones that, cumulatively, may also impact our lives for better or for worse. Regarding these daily choices President Gordon B. Hinckley said, "The course of our lives is seldom determined by great, life-altering decisions. Our direction is often set by the small, day-to-day choices that chart the track on which we run. This is the substance of our lives—making choices."[4]

How we choose to use our time each day is a choice. Elder Dallin H. Oaks said, "Consider how we use our time in the choices we make in viewing television, playing video games, surfing the Internet, or reading books or magazines. Of course it is good to view wholesome entertainment or to obtain interesting information. But not everything of that sort is worth the portion of our life we give to obtain it. Some things are better, and others are best. When the Lord told us to seek learning, He said, 'Seek ye out of the best of books words of wisdom' (D&C 88:118)."[5]

Happiness is also a choice. In 2 Nephi 2:25 we read, "Men are that they *might* have joy" (italics added). How we reflect our attitudes is a choice. So is keeping our covenants, staying chaste before marriage, being faithful to one's spouse, not watching inappropriate movies, and living the Word of Wisdom. In fact, almost everything we say and do and react to is a choice. It may not always be a conscious choice, but nevertheless it is a choice.

When we make unwise choices, we limit our options for the future. For instance, if a person chooses to view pornography or take drugs, over time he or she can become addicted and his or her ability to make the right choices diminishes. At that point, Satan will try to convince the addicted person that his or her agency is entirely gone. That is a lie! Through the Savior and His Atonement, *anyone* can heal, repent, and move on. Even if bad choices are made or serious sins committed, a person can receive the Lord's influence in his or her life and become empowered to make right choices again. The choice is ours—to choose Christ and His teachings; to choose happiness.

In his book *Man's Search for Meaning*, Viktor Frankl gives an account of his experiences in a concentration camp during the Holocaust. Regarding the choice we have over our attitudes

Frankl states, "We who lived in concentration camps can remember the men who walked through the huts comforting others, giving away their last piece of bread. They may have been few in number, but they offer sufficient proof that everything can be taken away from a man but one thing: the last of human freedoms—*to choose one's attitude in any given set of circumstances, to choose one's own way*" (italics added).[6]

Here is a man who lost his entire family and every material possession, even the clothes on his back. Yet, he chose to remain true to himself. Frankl continues, "Even though conditions such as lack of sleep, insufficient food and various mental stresses may suggest that the inmates were bound to react in certain ways, in the final analysis it becomes clear that the sort of person the prisoner became was the result of an inner decision and not the result of camp influences alone. Fundamentally, man can therefore; any man can, even under such circumstances, decide what shall become of him—mentally and spiritually."[7]

Frankl's words remind us that the old excuse of "I couldn't help myself" isn't an acceptable justification for bad behavior. We can help ourselves, and if we feel we can't, we'd better start calling upon Heavenly Father to help us improve our self-mastery!

As we live close to the Savior and His teachings, our desire to choose the right will increase. While living in a German concentration camp, Corrie ten Boom's sister Betsie chose to have an attitude of gratitude in the bleakest conditions. There is something to be said about learning from someone else's trials, which they went through during their own furnaces of affliction.

LEARNING TO TRUST IN THE LORD

In Corrie ten Boom's personal account of the experience, titled *The Hiding Place,* she describes how she and her sister miraculously smuggled a *Bible* into their living quarters. One night as the two sisters sat up reading the *New Testament,* they came across a scripture that spoke of giving thanks in all things.

Betsie and Corrie lived in a building that held 1,400 prisoners, although it was designed to hold only 400. Nine people shared their bunk for four. When fleas infested their small area and the buildings' toilets overflowed, Betsie chose to express gratitude. She was able to see a miracle in the fact that she and Corrie were located in the same camp and sleeping in the same bunk, and that because of the fleas, the guards left her and her sister alone.[8] Corrie ten Boom describes a conversation with Betsie as follows:

> "That's it, Corrie! That's His answer. 'Give thanks in all things, in all circumstances!' That's what we can do. We can start right now to thank God for every single thing about this new barracks!"
>
> I stared at her, then around me at the dark, foul-aired room.
>
> "Such as?" I said.
>
> "Such as being assigned here together."
>
> I bit my lip. "Oh yes, Lord Jesus."
>
> "Such as what you are holding in your hands."
>
> "I looked down at the *Bible.* "Yes! Thank You, dear Lord, that there was no inspection when we entered here! Thank You for all of the women, here in this room, who will meet You in these pages."

"Yes," said Betsie. "Thank You for the very crowding in here, since we are packed so close; that many more will hear!...Thank You," Betsie went on serenely, "for the fleas and for—

The fleas! This was too much. "Betsie, there's no way even God can make me grateful for a flea. Give thanks in all circumstances," she quoted.

"It doesn't say, 'in pleasant circumstances.' Fleas are part of this place where God has put us."[9]

Later in the book, the reader learns that many other women in this concentration camp were beaten and raped during their stay there. But because of the infestation of the fleas, the guards did not touch Betsie and Corrie. If that were my story, I would call it *The Miracle of the Fleas!*

Betsie's gratitude made me stop and think. In gloomy circumstances, however, I sometimes tend to be more like Laman and Lemuel than like Betsie or Nephi. From time to time, I'm guilty of murmuring and refusing to see the bigger picture. After my father passed away, I felt overwhelmed with grief, having lost both of my parents. Then I remember having a moment where even though I was sad, I knew that God lived and that the Atonement was real. In that moment, I chose to believe, I chose to hope, I chose to know God still had a plan for me. And I chose to move forward. Of course I still mourned and grieved; however, I strongly felt the peace that surpasses all understanding.

No matter the circumstances in our lives—a divorce, the death of someone we love, financial burdens, car problems, unemployment, or a quarrel with a family member or friend—

LEARNING TO TRUST IN THE LORD

we must step back and take a moment to choose to trust the Lord. At those times, we can ask ourselves, "What can I learn from this?" At that moment, we take a tremendous step of faith and will soon see the Lord's hand in our lives. (We'd also better get out our journals and record the lessons learned and the miracles that unfold, or we will forget them.) It is a *choice* to trust the Lord! It isn't always the easiest choice, but it is always the best one.

Now, I wasn't born yesterday. I also hear the negative voices and see the countless temptations that surround us. It is easy to be pessimistic in a world full of war and rumors of war. A person can't listen to the news for more than five minutes before there is a homicide of some sort reported or some other depressing news. Our society is inundated with suggestive sleaze. It is on billboards, on the Internet, on the television, and in many of the advertisements delivered to our homes. I'm certainly aware of all of this, but I try to choose to hope and to believe the words in Ether 12:4: "Wherefore, whoso believeth in God might with surety hope for a better world, yea, even a place at the right hand of God, which hope cometh of faith, maketh an anchor to the souls of men, which would make them sure and steadfast always abounding in good works being led to glorify God." So hope and faith in Jesus Christ can be our anchor to our souls!

As we are humble, exercise faith, and submit to the Lord's will, our ability to choose the right is increased. In his book, *To Draw Closer to God,* President Henry B. Eyring declared:

> "If doing right will bring you more knowledge of God, then of all the added knowledge of worth, one

of the most precious would be to know better the difference between right and wrong. I don't know what newspaper articles you read most recently...But you certainly have had this thought recently: How will I and those I love ever find our way through the increasing flood of filth and sin coming at us? I take courage from Joseph Smith's example and precept; listen for the voice of testimony, listen like a humble child, listen with the intent to obey, then obey, and then have confidence that your capacity to find the safe path—the ability to see and to choose the right—will grow at least in proportion to the confusion ahead."[10]

The Holy Ghost can help us make the right decisions. Some significant choices I've made in my life include getting baptized at age 17, serving a LDS mission, getting an education, moving to Utah from Oregon, and participating in international humanitarian expeditions to Vietnam, the Marshall Islands and other third world countries.

So many remarkable consequences have come from those choices. Most significantly, it has been an amazing journey to be a member of The Church of Jesus Christ of Latter-Day Saints. In 2008 I had the great opportunity of attending the temple and serving as proxy for my mother as my parents were sealed for eternity. Then my sister and I were sealed to our parents. It was such an amazing day, and I felt that my parents were there in spirit.

Now, I don't want to sound like I've never made a bad choice, because that couldn't be further from the truth. But I've tried to learn from my poor decisions, and through it all

I've learned for myself that the Lord will always be there for each of us. In the Hymn *Choose the Right,* we sing:

> "Choose the right! There is peace in righteous doing.
> Choose the right! There's safety for the soul.
> Choose the right in all labors you're pursuing;
> Let God and heaven be your goal.
> Choose the right! Choose the right!
> Let wisdom mark the way before.
> In its light, choose the right!
> And God will bless you ever more."[11]

I am grateful for the thirteenth Article of Faith which is: "We believe in being honest, true, chaste, benevolent, virtuous, and in doing good to all men; indeed, we may say that we follow the admonition of Paul—We believe all things, we hope all things, we have endured many things, and hope to be able to endure all things. If there is anything virtuous, lovely, or of good report or praiseworthy, we seek after these things." And I would add the following challenge with it:

CHALLENGE

Choose today to be honest, true, chaste, benevolent, and virtuous. Choose to do good to all men. Choose to hope all things and endure all things. Choose to seek after things that are virtuous, lovely, of good report, or praiseworthy. Think back in your life about the big choices you have made. In your journal write down the consequences and blessings that have come from them. If you have made some bad choices along the way—and I think we all have—write down what you learned about yourself at that time, or what you learned about the Lord's tender mercies.

Chapter 3

FOLLOWING THE COUNSEL OF OUR LEADERS

In Ohio in November 1931, Joseph Smith received the following revelation: "What I the Lord have spoken, I have spoken and I excuse not myself; and though the heavens and earth pass away, my word shall not pass away, but shall all be fulfilled, whether by mine own voice or by the voice of my servants, it is the same" (D&C 1:38). I am grateful for all the church leaders who have guided me throughout my life. So many teachers, bishops, and stake presidents have inspired me, and my mission president influenced my life in countless ways. We may not always know why someone is called to a church leadership position, but I am absolutely certain the Lord knows. And I have no doubt that we are far better off when we choose to follow the counsel of our church leaders. I am also grateful for the First Presidency and the Twelve Apostles.

Mary Jo, a friend and mentor, shared with me an experience about following the counsel of our church leaders. As a busy, young mother with three preschoolers she had been called along with her husband, Ted, to direct the first Northwest Dance Festival for the Church. This area covered 21 stakes in Washington, Oregon, and California. Mary Jo and Ted spent a great deal of time traveling to the stakes, overseeing the coordination of costumes, choreography of dances, etc.

One day, the bishop stopped by Mary Jo's home to see how she was doing. During his brief visit, Mary Jo's phone rang off the hook with people calling about the upcoming dance festival. The bishop then told Mary Jo that her children needed a mother at home and that she needed more time with them, so he planned to release her from her Young Women's calling. Mary Jo was devastated. She informed the bishop that she didn't want to be released; she loved the young women she worked with, and she felt like she could do it all. The release was made, and Mary Jo came to see the wisdom in the bishop's decision. She was able to spend time with her children at home as well as serve in the capacity with her husband as the director of the Northwest Dance Festival.

Another time when Mary Jo and Ted moved into a new ward and stake, Ted felt a little displaced and unneeded. Having just been released from serving as Stake Young Men's president in his former stake, Ted wanted to serve and felt he needed a calling. Their new bishop stopped by their home to say hello, and he counseled Ted to be careful to not be idle; to use this downtime—this time without a calling—to search, ponder, and read the scriptures. Ted followed this counsel and felt tremendously blessed by it.

When a friend of mine named Liz recently moved into a new ward, the bishop called her to be the Ward Primary president. Liz was taken back by this because she was single, worked full time, and was in school working towards a doctoral degree. Although she didn't know just how she could fulfill the calling or what she had to offer, she accepted it anyway. A short time later, as she taught the Sunbeams (three- and four-year-olds) that Heavenly Father and Jesus love them, each child raised his or her hand and asked, "Jesus loves me too?" As she witnessed their childlike faith and love, she knew she was right where she was supposed to be. She also discovered these children were fulfilling a need she didn't even know she had. Liz knew her bishop was inspired.

At age 26, Sarah had been married for one year when her husband suffered a brain hemorrhage and died. The day after he passed away, Sarah's bishop gave her a priesthood blessing that included some counsel that she was not prepared to hear: that she should marry again, and that both Heavenly Father and Sarah's husband wanted this for her. Initially, this counsel came as both a shock and a burden as Sarah couldn't even think of dating or remarrying. As time passed, she began meeting with a widow support group where she made many wonderful friends. Some of the women in the group indicated that they feel guilty for thinking about dating and marriage again. And while the idea was still sometimes difficult for Sarah, she had the benefit of knowing that this was what her husband—and her Heavenly Father—wanted for her. Sarah was grateful for a bishop who listened to the Spirit and gave her the specific counsel she needed.

A friend shared with me an experience that reinforced his desire to follow his church leaders in all things. During the time when this friend served as a stake president, a full-time missionary from his stake developed a rare form of cancer.

After medical exams and multiple hospital tests while in the mission field, the missionary returned home early to receive treatment. When he returned home, the young man married his girlfriend with both of them knowing his cancer would be terminal. This young couple visited with my friend—who was their stake president—several times during their brief marriage. Eventually, the couple telephoned him to tell him that the young man's final days were near. He visited them in their home and the young man passed away shortly thereafter.

Obviously, this was a difficult time for the young man's family. In his grief, the young man's father blamed the young man's mission president for not sending him home sooner. The father called his son's stake president and threatened to sue the Church for not sending his son home earlier. He said the Church should pay for the funeral, as he felt his son's death could have been prevented if he'd returned home sooner for treatment. These words weighed heavily on the stake president's mind, and he wasn't sure what to do. That same week, Elder Loren C. Dunn of the First Quorum of the Seventy visited the stake, and the stake president sought his counsel in regards to this difficult situation. Elder Dunn stated, "Whenever you are facing a decision between justice and mercy, you should always choose mercy." With that, the stake president called the grieving father and offered assistance with the funeral. He has never forgotten that counsel from one of the Lord's servants.

Another dear friend, who is like a mother to me, told me of the time her bishop counseled her to receive her temple blessings even though her husband was not a member of the Church. My friend was nervous about going to the temple because she thought it might create tension in her marriage, but the bishop assured her that if she went to the temple her marriage would be fine. Shortly after receiving this counsel, she took her husband to the Seattle Temple open house, which led to more conversations about the Church. Meanwhile, my friend kept thinking and praying about her bishop's counsel, yet still feared causing contention in the home.

A few years later, my friend's mother passed away, and my friend told her bishop that she wanted to have her mother's temple work done. The bishop reminded her that he'd felt for the last few years that she should receive her own temple endowment. Once again, he promised her that if she took this step, it would not hurt her marriage. And this time, the bishop told her that if she received her temple blessings it would actually make her marriage stronger and would encourage her husband to join the Church. The bishop explained that her going through the temple would be another example of her dedication to the Lord and His Church, and he promised her that all blessings she had been promised would be fulfilled. The bishop also told her that if she went through the temple, she would be more inspired as to how to help her husband and how to do her family history work.

The day my friend went to the temple, her husband gave her a beautiful pendant made from a circle of pearls. He said, "I felt strongly to give this to you and sustain you in your decision, and I am happy you want to take this step." He told her not to worry about him and that he supported her decision. Five years later, Peggy's husband was baptized into the Church. One year later, they were sealed for eternity, and their daughter was sealed to them.

I will never forget what I learned from the example of Elder Hazelton and Elder Jarnigan, the assistants to my mission president, while I served in my first area in Illinois. We were teaching the first discussion on the Prophet Joseph Smith and the First Vision to Larry and Arlene. Arlene knew the Church was true and would have been baptized that day if Larry would have supported her. Larry also knew what we taught was true, but in his fear to accept it, he stubbornly refused to admit what he knew. Refusing to give up on him, Elder Jarnigan asked Larry to kneel with us, to pray and to ask if Joseph Smith was a true prophet, and if he truly did see God the Father and His Son Jesus Christ. I will never forget the Spirit that filled the room when Larry asked this question. We all fought back the tears, and we all received a witness that Joseph Smith was a prophet. I'd known this before my mission, but now I really knew, with no doubt whatsoever. Many times on my mission after this we would ask those we were teaching to sincerely ask and seek to know the truth, and we promised that if they did this they would receive a witness. I was grateful for Elder Jarnigan's and Elder Hazelton's examples of faith and leadership.

As I prepared for dental hygiene school in Gresham, Oregon, I planned to take 21 credit hours, 18 of which were for science classes. Just the thought of taking extra classes in microbiology, anatomy, and physiology nearly overwhelmed me. So I informed my new bishop of the institute ward that I would love to visit teach and just hang low in the ward until the semester was over.

Imagine my surprise when the bishop called me in the very next week to ask me to be the Relief Society president!

LEARNING TO TRUST IN THE LORD

I told the bishop that I thought he was up in the night and that I would have to go home and pray about the calling. He said that would be okay, but that he knew the Lord had called me, and he explained that he would rather not delay setting me apart. So that very day I was sustained in sacrament meeting and then set apart. After the bishop set me apart, he gave me wise counsel that I think applies to anyone attending school. He promised me that I would have enough time to do whatever was required of me if I would never study on the Sabbath. This challenge was difficult at first, but to this day I have not studied on the Sabbath. And as I went to school and served as Relief Society president, I was blessed beyond my ability to describe, and I was able to accomplish all I needed in my studies and in my calling. The Lord truly is bound when we do what He says, and besides that, He loves to bless us.

Several years ago, I learned another great lesson from another bishop. Some bad choices by my brother-in-law made it necessary for my sister to seek a divorce. Watching my sister suddenly become a single mother of four was very painful for our entire family. And of course, the situation was nearly unbearable for my sister. She and I talked on the phone almost every day those first few months. I was in Utah and she was in Washington. After one particular phone conversation I remember feeling how heavy this financial and emotional burden was to her. In short, she was overwhelmed with the bills that regularly came due, and on top of everything, her clothes dryer broke. Because the Northwest has its share of rain, it was impossible to hang the wet clothes outside to dry, so my sister hung them inside the house. She said there were clothes everywhere—a sock here, a shirt there. After learning of her predicament, I felt helpless, so I prayed to know what to do. I decided that in addition to the other money I planned to send her, I would give her my fast offerings for the next few months.

The following Sunday I found my bishop and told him of my sister's dilemma, and then asked if it would be okay if I sent my fast offering to her in Washington. I will never forget what the bishop said to me. First, he acknowledged that my heart was in the right place. Then he said, "Michelle, I promise you that if you will give this sacred fast offering to the Lord, He will see to it that the money goes to those who need it." He continued, "I would even double your fast offering; the Lord knows who is in need." I remember thinking that if I gave the money directly to my sister, I would know for certain that she got it! But I followed my bishop's counsel and paid my fast offering to him.

What happened in the next week was in my eyes a fulfillment of these words from the *Old Testament:* "Prove me now herewith, saith the Lord of hosts, if I will not open you the windows of heaven and pour you out a blessing, that there shall be room enough to receive it" (Malachi 3:10). Specifically, my sister received a new clothes dryer from someone her ex-husband had previously home taught, and anonymous financial help came from several people. In addition, another family member called and said he would like to take over one of her bills for the next few months. It was remarkable to see such wonderful generosity. Of course, I don't think all this happened just because I paid a double

LEARNING TO TRUST IN THE LORD

fast offering. But I do believe my bishop was right when he said that the Lord knows who needs our fast offerings.

CHALLENGE

Think back to a time you received wise counsel from a bishop, stake president, Relief Society president, mission president, or other church leader. In your journal, write down the counsel and what happened when you followed it. If this person is still in your life, write and mail him or her a letter expressing your gratitude.

Chapter 4

WHEN THE SPIRIT SPEAKS, DON'T DELAY

Learning to feel and recognize the Spirit can sometimes be tricky. Warm fuzzies, goose bumps, clarity of thought, or feelings of peace are some of the ways I feel and recognize how the Holy Ghost speaks to me. President Boyd K. Packer taught:

> "The voice of the Spirit is described in the scriptures as being neither "loud" nor "harsh." It is "not a voice of thunder, neither…a voice of a great tumultuous noise." But rather, "a still voice of perfect mildness, as if it had been a whisper." And it can "pierce even to the very soul" and "cause [the heart] to burn." (3 Nephi 11:3; Helaman 5:30; D&C 85:6–7)…The Spirit does not get our attention by shouting or shaking us with a heavy hand. Rather it whispers. It caresses so gently that if we are preoccupied we may not feel it at all…Occasionally it will press just firmly enough for us to pay heed. But most of the time, if we do not heed the gentle

feeling, the Spirit will withdraw and wait until we come seeking and listening and say in our manner and expression, like Samuel of ancient times, "Speak [Lord], for thy servant heareth" (1 Samuel 3:10).[12]

Shortly after my baptism, I knew I wanted to serve a mission. That summer, two of my girlfriends left on their missions and I stayed in touch with both of them. Their letters inspired me and further increased my desire to serve a mission. When I turned 20, I assessed my finances and realized that in order to pay for my mission I would need to work for two more years. (I had lived on my own since age 17, and I hadn't saved a lot of money.)

One day, my friends Ted and Mary Jo Hodges (a couple with whom I had recently become acquainted) invited me to their home. Their daughter had just returned from her mission and they had recently sent a third child into the mission field. Having sent out three missionaries in three years, Ted and Mary Jo were filled with the missionary spirit.

When I met with them in their home, the Hodges said that they understood that I wanted to go on a mission and that I was saving to be able to pay for it. They explained that they felt strongly that I should go when the time was right—and they said the right time was at age 21. They then invited me to live with their family and save money for the next six months until my 21st birthday! I felt so humbled by this offer, and of course I immediately accepted it.

I had such an amazing experience living with this family. They had two sons, ages 10 and 15, with whom I developed close relationships. On numerous occasions, their youngest son David and I would read scriptures or stories together. His older brother Mike and I spoke at several firesides together; he was the youth speaker and I was the young adult speaker. We always spoke of the Atonement and what it meant to us. The Portland Oregon Temple was finished that summer, and Ted and Mary Jo had specific assignments to help with its completion. It was an exciting time to live with the Hodges, and I learned so much.

I worked for those six months, saved money, and received my mission call that summer. I departed for the Missionary Training Center in Provo, Utah one week after my 21st birthday. As mentioned earlier, my mother was diagnosed with terminal cancer when I had been on my mission only two months. Had I waited for my 22nd birthday, I probably would have never gone on a mission. The Lord knew this, and He knew I needed a mission experience in my life. My mom needed my mission experience too. I am grateful that the Hodges followed a prompting to help a sister get into the mission field at the appropriate time.

While serving on my mission in Decatur, Illinois, I was blessed for listening to the promptings of the Spirit. My companion and I were scheduled to follow up with an investigator named Rosalind on her *Book of Mormon* reading. Decatur is a great city where I had many wonderful experiences, but on this particular day we weren't in the safest part of town—and we especially shouldn't have been there after dark. We were about two houses away from Rosalind's when we both suddenly stopped walking. I told my companion that I had felt we should stop, and she said she'd received the same prompting. We asked Heavenly

Father, "Where should we be?" Immediately, a clear and quiet answer came, and we both knew that we should go home. We turned around and started walking home, about one minute later we heard gunshots from the direction of Rosalind's home and saw people scattering into the streets. After running for about 10 minutes, we reached our apartment. We called Rosalind, and the police officer who answered the phone indicated that there had been a homicide at the house and that Rosalind's cousin had been killed. If we had continued on to Rosalind's house, we would have been there when the shooting occurred, and perhaps we would have been victims as well. I'm eternally grateful for the Spirit's warning that evening.

On another occasion on my mission, while sleeping soundly, I was awakened by an audible voice saying something along the lines of, "Michelle, wake up, get up, get out of bed. WAKE UP!" I awoke and smelled gas. Now usually if you are being asphyxiated, you can't smell the gas, but I could smell it. My companion, Sister Kuehne, had a difficult time waking up. I shook her and we got up and called a member we knew could help us. He told us to get out of the apartment and to stay on the street until he arrived. It was in the middle of the night in the dead of winter in Burlington, Iowa, but we waited until the church member showed up. He turned off our gas and I believe we stayed with him and his family that night. He said it was a good thing that no one had walked by with a cigarette, or we would have not made it out of there. Once again, I was so grateful for a warning from the Spirit of the Lord!

While I served with Sister Kuehne in Burlington, Iowa, a talk tape circulated throughout the mission. On the tape,

WHEN THE SPIRIT SPEAKS, DON'T DELAY

Bill Carpenter related his conversion story. In short, Bill was converted while taking a break before his last year of schooling to become a Catholic priest. Following his conversion to the LDS Church, he served a mission without the approval of his family. While Bill was in the mission field, he found out that his father was terminally ill. Bill made the decision to stay on his mission. Obviously, Bill's story of being a convert and serving a mission with a nonmember family at home and a terminally ill parent mirrored my own situation. Bill mentioned on the tape that at the time of the recording, he was teaching large group meetings at the Missionary Training Center (MTC) in Provo.

I was at a crossroads on my mission. My mother's cancer had progressed and she was gravely ill, making it harder to exercise the faith to stay on my mission. Deciding to take a chance that Brother Carpenter still taught at the MTC, I wrote him a letter seeking advice. Should I stay on my mission or go home and be with my mother before she died? Also at this same time on my mission, one of my close friends, Kelly, was dying of pancreatic cancer at home and was going through a difficult time as well. When I sent Brother Carpenter the letter, I truly felt desperate.

Two weeks passed, during which time my friend Kelly passed away. Sister Kuehne and I had listened to Brother Carpenter's talk tape together on a preparation day (P-day). Early one morning, the phone rang. I answered it, and a gentleman asked for Sister Michelle Martin. Sister Kuehne, who stood beside me, could hear his voice. She looked at me and said, "That is Bill Carpenter!" I was shocked that he was calling me and wondered how he got my number.

LEARNING TO TRUST IN THE LORD

The miracle of all this was that my letter had reached him even though he no longer worked at the MTC. They forwarded his mail, but he had moved twice since working there. This particular morning he had awoken early and had gone outside to get the newspaper on the front porch. As he looked outside, he found my letter on his porch. He had no idea how it got there. When he read my letter, he felt strongly that he should call the MTC and find out who my mission president was. After doing so, he called President Burgess and received permission to contact me. I was so touched that Brother Carpenter would go through all that trouble to find me! One thing he said that I'll never forget: "It is when you step into the dark and let go and have faith, that the Lord will show you His miracle." He told me that he knew that somehow, someway, I would make it through all this and would be okay. We had a great talk. It was what I so desperately needed at this time with my mother's illness and Kelly's death. The Lord sent Brother Carpenter to help me stay on my mission. I have no doubt that God knows us and knows our specific needs! And I am so grateful Brother Carpenter did not delay acting on the Spirit.

After my mission, I returned to live in Portland, Oregon, with my friend Lora. An elderly couple lived in a house near our apartment and as we drove by we often noticed them working in the yard together. But one fall afternoon there was an ambulance in front of their home. We said to each other, "I hope they are okay." Shortly thereafter, we learned that the gentleman had a heart attack that day and passed away. Lora and I felt terrible for this lady, and we both felt strongly that we should do something for her. Because

Halloween was approaching, we took her a pumpkin with a cute face drawn on it and a note introducing ourselves, asking if there was anything we could do for her. We left it on her front porch.

A few days later while intently studying, I heard a knock at the door. Expecting a friend who planned to stop by to study, I was surprised to see Genie, the elderly neighbor lady. Through tears, she expressed her gratitude for our note and gift. I invited her into our little apartment and I felt blessed to be able to offer her a listening ear. The Spirit was very strong as we talked; I felt guided in what I should say to Genie. That was the beginning of a beautiful friendship between Genie, Lora, and me. Genie was from Germany. Her husband was forced to be a Nazi soldier, and when he escaped the military, the couple fled for America. They wanted nothing to do with the war and with Hitler's terrible genocide.

I really can't explain what happened that day in our little apartment in Portland, Oregon, but I know Heavenly Father knew that Genie needed us and that we needed her. We were so glad we followed the Spirit's prompting to share our love with her.

A few years later, I worked in Draper, Utah as a dental hygienist. One day, a female patient around 60 years old came into our office. Normally, I would only take a patient's blood pressure if he or she were taking more than one medication and might have medical complications. This particular patient didn't meet either criterion, but I felt impressed to take her blood pressure. A normal blood-pressure reading is about 120/80; hers was 223/135! I took it again with the same reading. My boss and I told her that under the circumstances we could not treat her that day, and we advised her to go to the emergency room or an urgent-care center. Later that day, we found out that she did need to receive medical treatment for her condition. I am so grateful that the Lord prompted me to take this patient's blood pressure. When the Spirit speaks, we should not delay.

On another occasion, I learned this lesson the hard way. During the 2002 Olympics in Salt Lake City, I volunteered five days a week, from 4:00 a.m. to 1:00 p.m. Because I also worked my regular job, the hours were starting to wear on me. One day, as I drove along State Street on my way home, I had an impression to turn right at the next traffic light. I was in the middle lane and the right lane was full of cars, so I didn't think I could change lanes in time. I thought, "Oh well." At the next traffic light a block away, I again felt that I should turn right. I remember thinking, "I don't need to turn right. That's the longer way home, and besides, it is more congested right now."

What happened next seemed like a dream. I proceeded through the light and was passing a small strip mall when suddenly a gunshot rang out and a bullet shattered my driver's side window! It startled me so much that I almost veered into another car. I pulled over and got out of the car with pieces of glass all over me. No one stopped to help me, and when I looked around, I saw nothing unusual. Traffic was very heavy, so I drove my car to an auto repair shop to see if I could get the window replaced, but I ended up having to wait until the next day. Fortunately, I was okay, but it was inconvenient to have to buy a new window and to go without one for a day, especially when it was so cold outside. The staff at the auto repair shop said that my window had probably been shot out by a BB gun or a paintball gun. I never found out who was responsible, but obviously I should have listened when the Spirit told me to turn right!

Another experience that illustrates the importance of listening to the Spirit occurred while I was a hostess at the Church Office Building. I was giving tours of the observation deck on the 26th floor. We would point out to visitors some of the sites that could be seen from the observation deck, such as the Salt Lake Temple, the Brigham Young Cemetery, and the Kennecott Copper Mine. My shift was Saturday mornings and on this particular morning the plantar fasciitis in my foot flared up. Because of the pain, I could barely walk, so I decided it would be best not to go in that day. As I was about to call my supervisor, I felt impressed not to, but to just go to the Church Office Building for my shift. I slipped on some brown, cushioned flip-flops from Hawaii because they were the only thing that helped ease the pain.

While I was on the 26th floor, another hostess came by with a young man and woman in their 20's. The young woman looked at my shoes and asked, "Have you been to Hawaii?" I told her I had and she proceeded to tell me that she had attended BYU–Hawaii and had worked at the Polynesian Cultural Center. This young woman's name was Nancy and she introduced me to her friend, Amaitsa. Amaitsa was an African man from Kenya. The two had met on an African educational website while Nancy was at

BYU-Hawaii. Nancy had been teaching Amaitsa about the Church and was in Salt Lake City for the first time—he had come to see Temple Square. Amaitsa told me that he was currently living in the Portland, Oregon area. I told him I was from the Portland area and asked specifically where he lived. As it turned out, Amaitsa lived in my old area, near my friends Ted and Mary Jo Hodges. At that time, Ted was serving as a bishop.

I asked Amaitsa if he had taken the missionary discussions before and he explained that he had started a couple years earlier but never finished. When I asked him why he never finished taking the discussions and why he hadn't been baptized, he said he wasn't sure but that perhaps he hadn't been ready. I told Amaitsa about my friends, the Hodges, and said that I would call them and tell them I had met him, had given him their phone number, and that he would be calling them. I encouraged Amaitsa to call them that night or the next day when he flew back to Portland. As soon as my shift was over, I called Ted and Mary Jo and told them about Amaitsa. They laughed and informed me that this was perfect timing because the next night, which would be Sunday, the missionaries were scheduled to come over for dinner! "Amaitsa can meet them then," Ted said enthusiastically. I said to Ted, "Let's pray he calls." We were all excited about this opportunity. I was elated to hear the next day that Amaitsa had called and had gone to their home for dinner and had the first discussion.

A little over two weeks later, Nancy and I flew up to Portland to speak at Amaitsa's baptism! It was a wonderful experience. The Lord was in the details every step of the way. The Hodges had a young man named Patrick living with them.

WHEN THE SPIRIT SPEAKS, DON'T DELAY

Patrick had returned home from his mission a week before they all met Amaitsa. He played an integral part in Amaitsa's conversion, sitting in on the discussions and helping out a great deal. Nancy and I are now kindred friends. Amaitsa has since moved to Salt Lake City, married in the Salt Lake Temple, started a family, and is doing very well. I am so happy the Spirit told me to serve my shift that morning, because I can't imagine my life without this incredible experience and these incredible people.

Let me share one last personal experience about following the promptings of the Spirit. On December 27, 2006, I wrote the following in my journal:

> "Dad had another heart attack…what a whirlwind of emotions! In a nutshell, he has had dialysis three times in the coronary care unit and they have pumped three pounds of fluid out of his lungs twice and six pounds of fluid the third time. Dad's heart is now functioning at 15% right now, and the doctor does not expect his heart to improve.
>
> Yesterday, I felt so strongly I was supposed to talk to dad, so I called to talk to his nurse (ICU patients don't have access to a telephone). The nurse said dad was very down in the dumps and very sad. She also said he was anxious about his condition. When I told the nurse that I wished I could talk to him, she said, "You can. I'll transfer the phone call to a portable phone and take it in to him." Moments later, I was talking with my dad, and we had a marvelous conversation. I asked him if he was feeling down and he said he was concerned

about the doctor's prognosis and was apprehensive about what was going to happen. I asked him if he was scared about the future—about dying. He said he was and wasn't sure what was going to happen to him.

I had a very tender conversation on the phone with him. I told him that his spirit would continue to live after he died. I told him he would have a great reunion with his parents and with his brother, and that they were aware of him at this time and all he was going through. The spirit of truth was felt and the feeling of love was so strong. I tried very hard not to let dad know I was crying. I tried to stay strong but was not able to. I cried pretty hard. His reply to all of this was, "Honey, I hope you're right." I said, "Dad, I know I am right." He was very pensive and thoughtful with this information and witness of life after death.

I also felt prompted to tell him about the day I got off my mission and saw mom for the first time. I told him that she had hugged me and pulled me in a room and asked me, "What is going to happen to my body when I die?" I told him at first I was not prepared to hear this question from one of my parents. I was in no way prepared to accept the possibility of her dying. I told him it was a few days later while mom was in the hospital that we had the same conversation that he and I were having at this time on the phone. I told him at that time that I explained to her what I was explaining to him.

Dad was very touched with the thought of being able to see his parents and his brother, my Uncle

Bill, again. It was a very emotional phone call, yet very tender. I am so grateful for the opportunity I had to have this amazing conversation with my dad. This is a conversation we never would have had even two months prior to this time. He wasn't prepared before then. I am still not sure why the timing of everything happened the way it did; however, I know the Lord knows."

CHALLENGE

Take time to recognize the feelings of the Spirit and to act upon them. In your journal, record a time when you followed the promptings of the Spirit. Make sure you include the details of the situation. And don't forget to thank Heavenly Father for the companionship of His Spirit. I also challenge you to bear your testimony, as often as possible, to your family, friends, and neighbors. So many people are seeking for answers to life's profound questions, and we're so blessed to have those answers.

Chapter 5

STAND STILL IN THE FURNACE OF AFFLICTION

One of my favorite stories from the *Old Testament* is about the fiery furnace and about Shadrach, Meshach, and Abed-nego found in the book of Daniel:

> Shadrach, Meshach, and Abed-nego, answered and said to the king, O Nebuchadnezzar, we are not careful to answer thee in this matter.
> If it be so our God whom we serve is able to deliver us from the burning fiery furnace, and he will deliver us out of thine hand, O king.
> But if not, be it known unto thee, O king, that we will not serve thy gods, nor worship the golden image which thou hast set up.
> Then was Nebuchadnezzar full of fury, and the form of his visage was changed against Shadrach, Meshach, and Abed-nego; therefore he spake, *and commanded that they should heat the furnace one seven times more than it was wont to be heated...*

And these three men, Shadrach, Meshach, and Abed-nego, fell down bound into the midst of the burning fiery furnace.

Then Nebuchadnezzar the king was astonished, and rose up in haste, and spake, and said unto his counselors, "Did not we cast three men bound into the midst of the fire?" They answered and said unto the king, True, O king.

He answered and said, Lo, *I see four men loose, walking in the midst of the fire, and they have no hurt; and the form of the fourth is like the Son of God.*

Then Nebuchadnezzar came near to the mouth of the burning fiery furnace, and spake, and said, Shadrach, Meshach, and Abed-nego, ye servants of the most high God, come forth, and come hither. Then Shadrach, Meshach, and Abed-nego, came forth of the midst of the fire.

And the princes, governors, and captains, and the king's counselors, being gathered together, saw these men, upon whose *bodies the fire had no power, nor was a hair of their head singed, neither were their coats changed, not the smell of fire had passed on them.* (Daniel 3:16–19, 23–27; italics added)

Like me, you probably enjoy sitting around a campfire with family or friends. And when you do this, doesn't the smell of the campfire remain in your hair and your clothing until you wash them? So when Shadrach, Meshach, and Abed-nego were thrown into the fiery furnace, how could the fire have NO power to hurt them or to destroy them?

LEARNING TO TRUST IN THE LORD

Why had the smell of fire passed over these brave Israelites? I believe it is because they chose to do as the Lord has counseled even in our day, "Be still, and know that I am God" (D&C 101:16). Let us trust the Lord even though we can't see very far down the path in front of us. Trust Him, even though we can't see what is on the other side of our Red Sea, and submit our will to God's.

At BYU Women's Conference, Wendy Watson Nelson addressed this very subject, "May I suggest that some of the most heart-wrenching, discouraging events in our lives—from which we long to be set free—are actually designed to prepare us with the very skills and understanding the Lord needs us to have. As we draw closer to the Lord and put our total trust in Him, in His power, and in His timing, we can leave our fires of affliction more pure, more refined, and with more skills and understanding, instead of leaving having been burnt to a crisp!"[13]

When I found out about my mother's cancer diagnosis while on my mission, I learned about the Savior's love and healing balm during our afflictions. It was the week before Christmas and I felt something wasn't right at home. This particular morning, my companion and I had set out on foot to contact our investigators because there was a tremendous amount of snow and our car was buried deep in it. When we were about a block from home, we realized that we had forgotten the blue daily planner. (If you've been on a mission you know you can't live without the blue planner!)

We went back to our apartment and as we walked in the door the telephone rang. My stomach turned; I knew it was for me. Sister Stock answered the phone, then turned toward me and said, "They asked for Michelle." I took the phone and said hello. Then I heard my sister Mattye state gravely, "You may want to sit down Michelle." I asked, "Is it Mom?" She wondered, "How did you know?" and I answered, "I don't know! I just know something is wrong." She proceeded to tell me that our mother had cancer, and that it had spread from fluid in her lungs to her reproductive organs. Mattye said the prognosis was bad and that mom would have a radical hysterectomy and then start chemotherapy treatments. After Mattye gave me a few more details, we agreed to talk on Christmas Day.

When I hung up the phone, Sister Stock came over and put her arms around me. Emotionally, I felt like someone had just hit me in the head with a golf club. I went to the bathroom and threw up, then told my companion I needed to be alone and went into the bedroom. Because of the terribly cold, snowy weather, we had problems with our phone and couldn't get in touch with our mission president. In despair, I cried as though my heart would literally break, then laid on the bed for what felt like eternity. My companion came into the room and put her arm around me and said, "Sister Martin, you are going to make it through this. We are going to make it through this together with the Savior's help." She hugged me and left the room.

I slipped off the bed onto my knees and started to pray. I prayed like I had never prayed before, pouring my soul out to Heavenly Father, pleading for Him to please help me. I remember looking up and seeing on the wall above my bed a picture of Christ in the Garden of Gethsemane. After a time, I felt as if His loving arms were wrapped around me, comforting me, letting me know that no matter what happened, I would be okay because of His Atonement. He truly was bearing my grief and carrying my sorrows (Isaiah 53:4), and I knew I could face whatever was ahead of me with the Savior's and Heavenly Father's help.

You might be at a place in life that you didn't think you'd be five or ten years ago. You may feel overwhelmed with life, even a little disappointed. Perhaps you are dealing with unemployment, a lack of relationships, feeling stuck in a job you don't want to do anymore, or even dealing with a recent divorce or the loss of a loved one. You may not feel that you're where you're supposed to be. But you can find out if you are on the right path. Ask the Lord to let you know. He will help you be right where He needs you. The key is to trust even though you can't see ahead, to lay your will on the altar of the Lord and to expect great things. In a stake conference that I attended, President Henry B. Eyring said, "Heavenly Father wants great things for us too."[14]

In February 2007, I had another experience in the furnace of affliction when I had to deal with the loss of my father from cancer. Having now lost both my parents, there were moments in the first few days and weeks after he died that I thought, "This is too much to bear! I can't do this on my own. I can't carry this burden!" However, I knew the burden would not go away—I knew that I must go through it. When I prayed—and that was often—I asked Heavenly Father to strengthen my shoulders so they could bear my burdens. And through the Holy Ghost, I discovered that I had much to learn from this particular burden. The Lord wanted this trial to sanctify and purify me, and I knew I must choose to allow it to do so. I felt so vulnerable at this time in my life; yet, the Lord carried my burdens and I was able to place my full confidence and trust in Him. During a talk at BYU–Idaho, Elder David A. Bednar said:

> "Consider the example of Mosiah 24 as Alma and his people are being persecuted by Amulon. As recorded in verse 14, the voice of the Lord came to these good people in their affliction and indicated: "And I will also ease the burdens which are put upon your shoulders, that even you cannot feel them upon your backs." Now if I had been one of Alma's people and received that particular assurance, my response likely would have been, "I thank thee, and please hurry!" But notice in verse 15 the process the Lord used to lighten the burden: "And now it came to pass that the burdens which were laid upon Alma and his brethren were made light; the Lord did strengthen them that they could bear up the burdens with ease, and they did submit cheerfully and with patience to all the will of the Lord." Brothers and sisters, what was changed in the episode? It was not the burden that changed; the challenges and difficulties of persecution were not immediately removed from the people. But Alma and his followers were strengthened, and their increased capacity and strength made the burdens they bore lighter."[15]

While going through adversity, we should not ask, "Why me?" but rather, "What can I learn from this?" Our Heavenly Father lives and loves us—this I know. I know that Jesus Christ is the Savior of the world, the Prince of Peace, and the only one that can give us the peace that passeth all understanding (Philippians 4:7). I know Joseph Smith is the Prophet of the Restoration, and that the *Book of Mormon* is the word of God. I'm grateful for the furnaces of affliction in life that can have no power to destroy us unless we choose to let them. In fact, these trials are meant to teach us, to sanctify us, and to purify us. It is my prayer that all of us can "be still and know God lives" (D&C 101:16).

CHALLENGE

Write in your journal daily, and be especially vigilant to write during times of adversity. The thoughts and feelings from your own journal can help you with trials that you will pass through later. Reading my journal entries about my mother's death helped me get through the difficult period that followed my father's passing.

Chapter 6

IT'S NEVER TOO LATE TO PRAY

We are never beyond the reach of our Heavenly Father and we are always in need of cultivating a relationship with Him. One day on my mission, while serving in Decatur, Illinois, my companion and I cut through a neighborhood that was probably off-limits for sister missionaries because of crime, drugs, and just plain dangerous conditions. As we walked through the neighborhood, we saw a woman who appeared to be several months pregnant, sitting in a rocking chair on the porch of an old, run-down house. She held a cigarette, and we watched her take a few puffs from it. Two toddlers darted around the front yard, which was overgrown with tall grass and weeds. My companion and I decided to find out about this woman and her story. We walked up the cracked concrete driveway and approached her. We introduced ourselves to the woman, who said that her name was Cheryl and that she was 27 years old. She had five or six children, each with a different father, and the father of the child she was pregnant with was in prison for drug use.

LEARNING TO TRUST IN THE LORD

After we talked with Cheryl for a long time, she disclosed that she had been sexually abused as a child. Ironically, it was a pastor that abused her. Consequently, Cheryl had some reservations about discussing religion. She also admitted that she didn't know how to read. We spent the rest of the afternoon talking with Cheryl about prayer and telling her that we knew Heavenly Father loved her and cared about her life. While we were visiting with Cheryl, a friend of hers named Vicki dropped by. Vicki had been staying in a woman's shelter because she had been a victim of domestic violence. She had left her baby with Cheryl overnight while she stayed at the shelter, and she said that the baby was inside Cheryl's house. We'd been talking for a long time on the porch, so we decided to go in and see if the baby was okay, guessing that Cheryl had been sitting on the porch all day, leaving the baby unattended.

As we entered the house, there were no lights on, just sunlight slivering through the curtain windows. We saw cockroaches climbing all over the walls and floor. I walked across the room and started to smell the horrible stench of urine. As I approached the baby, the smell got stronger. The baby whimpered softly, but it stopped crying as I picked him up. His clothing was soaked with urine, so I took him into the bathroom, and as I turned on the light, roaches scattered everywhere. I took the diaper off the baby and it looked as if mold or something had formed in the diaper. As I turned on the water to try to bathe the baby, a horde of roaches came out of the pipes.

After we tried to care for the baby, my companion and I talked with Cheryl and Vicki again, asking if we could teach them how to pray. Cheryl said she wasn't sure if there was a

God, and that if there was He didn't love her because of all she had done in her life and because of what happened to her when she was a little girl. We told Cheryl to just pretend there is a God, to just pretend He is there, and to just pretend He will answer. We taught Cheryl the basic steps of prayer, and she agreed to try to pray. The four of us knelt in Cheryl's living room after pulling the drapes to let in some light. Cheryl started, "Heavenly Father, are you there?" Immediately, we all felt the Spirit so strongly, even with cockroaches crawling all over us. Cheryl went on, "Do you love me even though I haven't lived the best life?" We could all feel the power of God's love in that room, and I don't know if I've felt it more strongly since. It was amazing, and all four of us had tears in our eyes as the Spirit bore witness of God's love for Cheryl.

For the next two weeks, we visited with Cheryl for about an hour a day. We read from the *Book of Mormon* with her, we washed her children's hair and cut it, and we cleaned her house. We found weevils in the baby bottles, and so we boiled them. One day we had zone conference (a meeting with a large group of missionaries) and other appointments, so we weren't able to visit Cheryl. The next day was Sunday, so we had church meetings in addition to several appointments. We kept feeling that we should go see Cheryl, but we just didn't make it that day. On Monday, our preparation day, we walked to Cheryl's house and found an official-looking note on the door that said, "UNFIT FOR HUMAN OCCUPANCY." A neighbor told us that Child Protective Services had come and taken the children and then condemned the house. We never found out where Cheryl went, and we never saw her again. But

LEARNING TO TRUST IN THE LORD

I'm so grateful we had the opportunity to teach her that she was a child of God and that He loved her—and to teach her how to pray.

Elder Richard G. Scott stated, "Prayer is a supernal gift of our Father in Heaven to every soul. Think of it: the absolute Supreme Being, the most all-knowing, all-seeing, all-powerful personage, encourages you and me, as insignificant as we are, to converse with Him as our Father…Humble, trusting prayer brings direction and peace."[16]

I learned another great lesson about prayer. At work one day, I had a heated discussion with a coworker. This occurred at the end of the week; consequently, I stewed over it all weekend. I was very angry at her. I knew it wasn't going to get better unless I earnestly sought the Lord's help, so on Sunday I prayed hard that things would be okay at the office the next day.

Monday morning came and I dreaded going in to work, I started my morning scripture reading with heavy thoughts. Of course, the two things I came across were to trust in the Lord in all things (Alma 5:13) and to love and pray for my enemies (3 Nephi 12:44). Not that my coworker was my enemy, but we'd certainly had contention. At first I decided I couldn't pray about the situation anymore, but then I humbled myself and began to pray. An interesting thing happened, I felt prompted to pray to know how Heavenly Father felt about this coworker! This prayer was answered immediately as I had a glimpse of Heavenly Father's love for her and for me as well. When I went to work and shared this with my coworker, we hugged each other and shed plenty of tears. It didn't matter what happened after that because I knew how Heavenly Father felt about her.

Lucy Mack Smith, one my favorite women from Church history, taught a powerful lesson on the influence of a mother's prayer. In her book, *The History of Joseph Smith, by His Mother,* Lucy tells how Joseph and Hyrum suffered from cholera during their journey with Zion's Camp. Lucy writes, "Hyrum sprang to his feet and exclaimed, 'Joseph, we shall return to our families. I have had an open vision, in which I saw mother kneeling under an apple tree; and she is even now asking God, in tears, to spare our lives, that she may again behold us in the flesh. The Spirit testifies, that her prayers, united with ours, will be answered."[17] Because they had seen their mother regularly exercising faith and praying to God, Joseph and Hyrum had full confidence that her prayer on their behalf would be answered.

In October 1999, I went on an oral health humanitarian mission to the Marshall Islands. Our team consisted of four oral health-care professionals, a nursing student, and an interpreter, who was also a medical student. On our first day on the island of Majuro, we met with the elementary school principal (who spoke some English) to receive orientation regarding the week's events. While sitting in the principal's "office," which consisted of a chair and a small desk, I noticed a scuba tank hanging just outside his door and asked him what it was for. He said he used it as the school bell, so I asked if I could ring it. He consented, giving me a coconut and demonstrating that I should bang it on the scuba tank. As I did so, it made a very loud sound, and all the kids immediately scurried into their classrooms.

I noticed that the scuba tank was very heavy, and I later learned that an empty scuba tank can weigh nearly fifty pounds depending on its size. Thinking of my "walking through the Red Sea" analogy where I would figuratively carry a backpack full of scuba gear, I started to realize just how heavy all this equipment can be. Carrying around scuba gear—which includes a scuba tank, fins, a mask, and a wet suit—could be very heavy, especially when you don't even need it. Remember, we are trying to walk through our Red Seas with faith, and Heavenly Father will not forsake us by letting the walls of water fall down on us. I believe there are many times in life when we carry burdens that we need not carry, when we need to let go and give our burdens to the Lord that they may be light. Prayer is one of the greatest ways we can exercise our faith in Heavenly Father and in His Son Jesus Christ.

For almost 12 years I worked as a dental hygienist, and due to the physical strain of the work, I developed two bone spurs in my right shoulder. Because of the tremendous amount of pain caused by working as a dental hygienist, I finally realized I needed to change occupations—and quickly. The process, however, was not quick. Long-suffering was a word I came to know well during this time. Being in my mid-thirties, I wanted to be married and have a family, as most of my friends did. So as I considered what I could do for a new career, I tried to make peace with myself and simply make sure I was where the Lord needed me. I decided to attend graduate school and further my education so that I would be in a better position to help others and in a better position to provide for myself.

It was around this time, as I dealt with my shoulder problems and decided to change occupations, that my father was diagnosed with his cancer and passed away a few months later. Although I was able to spend a little time with him before he died, this was, of course, a very difficult time. I was drained both emotionally and physically as I struggled to cope with losing my father. My pain in my shoulder continued to progressively get worse. Through this time I did not feel like I was in a rut; I felt even worse, like I was in limbo. While I knew I was being prepared for something, I just wasn't sure what it was or how I should proceed. I was certainly grateful for my dental hygiene position, and I continued to work through the pain in my shoulder while also searching diligently for a new job.

Eventually, I began receiving job offers that on paper seemed perfect for me, but somehow I knew I shouldn't accept them. I knew the Lord didn't want me to take a job—any job—just to work. Instead, I knew I had to do something I felt passionate about. I recently had a heart-to-heart talk with a friend and a mentor. This friend challenged me to write a list of what makes my spirit soar and then make a separate list of what I want in life. She then challenged me to ask Heavenly Father how best to fulfill the measure of my creation. This was a turning point for me because my list of what makes my spirit soar became my measuring stick of how to direct my life. When a job came my way, I would ask myself, "Does this make my spirit soar?"

Several years ago, because my mother and other friends of mine had succumbed to cancer, I volunteered in the infusion room at the Huntsman Cancer Institute in Salt Lake City. Since that time, I've thought it would be great to be an effective educational catalyst for cancer, and that if I ever changed jobs I would want to work at the Huntsman

LEARNING TO TRUST IN THE LORD

Cancer Institute. The minute the Huntsman Cancer Institute posted a cancer information specialist position, I knew that was what I was supposed to do and where I was supposed to be. I hoped so much to get an interview for the job. About a month after I applied for the job, a woman from another company called and offered me an excellent position with great income and benefits.

Once again, this was logically a great opportunity for me, since my shoulder pain was almost unbearable as I continued to work in dental hygiene. I remember praying and pleading, "Heavenly Father, I know that You know how much my shoulder hurts. I know that You know where I am supposed to work and where You need me the most. Please lead me to where Thou wouldst have me be." During this time, I attended the temple every week. The week I received the job offer, I went to the temple and cried and prayed and pleaded with the Lord for His guidance, asking Him to deliver me from this circumstance. I prayed that He would bear up my shoulders that they could bear this burden of having such an unsettled spirit and feeling anxious about my future. I prayed that I would learn what He wanted me to learn during this time of uncertainty. Even though I was still distressed about my situation, I felt "the peace of God, which passeth all understanding" (Philippians 4:7). I didn't know how this circumstance would change, but I knew that God loved me, He was aware of me and that I was not alone.

I asked the representative from the other company if I could think about the job offer and call her back in 24 hours, although I knew I didn't really need 24 hours. I called her the next day and explained that I was grateful for the opportunity but would have to decline. I even told her I felt like I should be doing something else. She asked me, "Like what?" I told her I wanted to teach cancer awareness at the Huntsman Cancer Institute and that I had applied for a position there. She asked if I had an interview scheduled with them. I told her I did not, but I knew it was where I was supposed to be. She was very kind, but I knew she was thinking, "Okay, good luck with that." I remember hanging up the phone and thinking to myself, "I hope I didn't just pass up a good opportunity. Maybe I should just take it to have the benefits and give my shoulder a break." As I thought this, I immediately felt the Spirit's reproof, "Michelle, you are being true to what you said, that you won't take a job just to take a job. Remember you want to do what makes your spirit soar. You keep asking me to lead you where I need you the most. Have faith!"

A few days later, I took a sister from our ward a meal after surgery, and she asked me how my job search was coming along. I told her I had applied for a job at the Huntsman Cancer Institute and that I couldn't get a contact name to get an interview. She said, "Oh, I know so-and-so. You can call him!" Well, it just so happens that I knew him too, but I didn't know he worked there. The very next day I called him and asked him about the job. He gave me the name and number of a woman to call in regards to the position I wanted, and he said I could use his name when speaking to her. I called her, left a message, and heard back from her within five minutes. She asked me to come in for an interview the next day! In my mind this was a miracle, and how grateful I was for it. Two weeks later, I was offered and accepted a job as a cancer information specialist at the Huntsman Cancer Institute, and I know this was exactly where I was supposed to be at that time.

As I recently prepared to teach a lesson in Relief Society, I went back to my list of what makes my spirit soar, and my list of what I want to do with my life regarding a career. I had written two things that I didn't remember writing: I wanted to work for the Church's humanitarian welfare program or for the Huntsman Cancer Institute (HCI) helping increase cancer awareness. I wrote this almost nine months before I started the job with HCI! Without a doubt, I know that Heavenly Father prepared me for this opportunity and directed me towards it. And while I was overwhelmed with all I needed to learn for my new job, I was learning to be patient with myself as I tried to help people suffering from cancer.

I decided to teach my Relief Society sisters what my friend had taught me, and to give them the same challenges she gave me. So I challenged each sister to make a list of what makes her spirit soar and to make a list of what she wants in life. I also challenged each sister to kneel and pray vocally twice a day, asking Heavenly Father to help her know how best to fulfill the measure of her creation. I explained what I had found out for myself—that when I follow the counsel to kneel and pray vocally, I tend to pray more from my heart rather than just my mind. Most lifelong church members have probably been taught to do this, but since I didn't grow up in the Church, I didn't have this advantage. I remember hearing that it was better to pray out loud, but I never really took it to heart until my friend gave me the challenge. A week before my lesson, I asked three sisters in my Relief Society to accept the challenge and then report back as part of my lesson. I also began praying aloud twice a day on my knees. Here are the results of the challenge:

- We prayed more earnestly and with more meaning. We felt specifically directed as to what to pray for.
- We each felt Heavenly Father's individual love for us. One sister said she instantly felt the Spirit when she prayed vocally.
- We experienced increased spiritual awareness and consciousness.
- We felt more humble during prayer.
- We found more purpose in prayer.
- One sister was inspired in her relationship with her spouse and her children.
- One sister was inspired in her relationship with a sibling and felt strongly that Heavenly Father cared about that eternal relationship.
- Each sister felt more calm and more at peace.
- One sister was inspired to write a letter to someone in the middle of the night and was guided in what to say.
- One sister was inspired how to use her talents and how specifically to help others use their talents.
- All sisters were inspired to make spiritual decisions—not just logical decisions.

The list went on and on. This experience was truly amazing, and I felt honored to be an instrument in Heavenly Father's hands in helping these sisters receive inspiration and peace. I am so grateful for vocal prayer. According to the Bible Dictionary, prayer is a form of work. Each sister I asked in advance to do this experiment said that praying vocally was hard and a lot of work. Even the great prophet of our dispensation, Joseph Smith, had watched his parents pray vocally but had not prayed vocally himself until the spring of 1820.[18]

For a long time, I struggled with vocal prayer, but now I count it as one of my greatest blessings. Prayer is a form of work, but it is definitely worth it.

When I gave the "prayer challenge" to my Relief Society sisters, I extended a caution as well—the same caution that my friend had given me. It is this: Satan does not want us to know who we are. He does not want us to learn our missions in life or how we can accomplish them. Unlike us, the adversary remembers everything from the pre-existence, so he knows our amazing potential for good—and just how powerful we can be when directed by the Holy Ghost. So we must keep praying and asking Heavenly Father how we can best fulfill the measure of our creation. There is absolutely nothing we can't accomplish with the Lord on our side. Patricia T. Holland gave the following challenge regarding prayer:

> "Find a private place and kneel comfortably and calmly in the center of the room. For a few moments say nothing, just think of Him. Just kneel there and feel the closeness of His presence, His warmth, His peace. With humility, express your gratitude for every blessing, every good thing you enjoy. Share with Him your problems and fears. Talk to Him about each

one and pause long enough to receive His counsel. I promise that you will learn His shoulders are broad enough for your burdens.

However, rolling our entire bundle of burdens onto His shoulders is not a simple matter; it requires a majestic leap of faith. Sometimes when we are the loneliest or when we feel the greatest hurt is precisely the time when we feel God is not there, the very time when we feel utterly abandoned by Him and by others. But such willingness to trust that He will comfort us, especially in difficult times—such willingness to make that leap of faith toward His embrace when we are least certain of His presence—could well be the most monumental single step of our lives. When we hand our fears and frustrations to Him in absolute confidence that He will help us resolve them, when in this way we free our heart and mind and soul of all anxiety, we find a rather miraculous way that He can instill within us a whole new perspective. He can fill us with "that joy which is unspeakable and full of glory" (Helaman 5:4)."[19]

CHALLENGE

Take the time to pray vocally more often, on your knees if you can. Be specific in both your gratitude and your petitions. As you do this, your love for Heavenly Father and Jesus Christ will increase, and you will learn how much They love you! It is only through prayer that you can truly learn

LEARNING TO TRUST IN THE LORD

how to fulfill the measure of your creation. You have many things to accomplish while on the earth, and many blessings await you if you will just ask for them and live worthy of them. If you don't believe me, just read and pray about your patriarchal blessing.

Chapter 7

LEARNING TO LAUGH AT YOURSELF

In case you haven't served a Church mission, let me just share something with you; many not-so-serious things happen in the mission field! The first Sunday on my mission I was welcomed with a severe snowstorm and a seriously cold wind. My companion and I walked into the church building and hurried to remove and hang up our coats. My companion met our investigator in the chapel while I took off the scarf I'd wrapped several times around my neck and head.

Knowing I would meet the Elders in my district that day—and knowing the Lord had called me to serve in this particular ward in His vineyard—I was probably more than a little nervous. In addition, our mission office was located in this city (Peoria, Illinois), so there were several missionary companionships in the ward. I recall thinking as I walked into the chapel, "These are the members whose homes we'll be in, and I will teach their friends."

At any rate, after removing my scarf I hurried into the chapel. The meeting was just starting, so I quickly found my companion and our investigator and sat down next to them. The bishop was talking, but somehow I couldn't hear him at all! I wondered why he didn't turn on the microphone or if it was broken or something. I was wearing a new outfit that I'd purchased for my mission, and I felt like a crisp, new sister missionary. Then, I noticed my companion looking at me with raised eyebrows and a quizzical smile. Suddenly, and with great mortification, I realized I hadn't removed my BIG, pink, fluffy earmuffs. So much for trying to make a great first impression!

Another time in the same part of my mission, my companion and I were tracting in even colder weather. In fact, the conditions were blizzard-like. We stepped up onto a porch and knocked on the door. Being tired from the cold, I leaned my head back on a small pillar that helped hold up the porch. A gentleman answered the door and told us to go away, then he shut the door. Suddenly the pillar, which was obviously not very sturdy, broke—and I fell backward off the porch into some bushes. My big coat and dress flipped up over my head, exposing my winter thermals. I thought, "Oh, my goodness!" I realized I was stuck in the bushes on top of the post. My companion and I both laughed hysterically. With my head deep in the snow-covered bushes and my feet in the air, I couldn't get up, so my companion stepped off the porch and trudged through the snow to help me flip over. While I hurt from the fall and was miserably cold, my companion and I laughed the whole way home. (By the way, the owner of the home must have heard the commotion, because he opened the door and told us to get off his porch, not even offering to help.)

LEARNING TO LAUGH AT YOURSELF

Regarding laughter, Elder Neal A. Maxwell once said, "How wonderful it is to see those whose sense of humor includes the capacity to see themselves and their frailties laughingly—not into the chronic, self-deprecating, biting way. Those who can see themselves and their incongruities with smiles (not sarcasm) suggest to the rest of us that they have an inner security, and this encourages the rest of us to take heart in a world in which too many of us are much too serious about ourselves and in which too much of the laughter is nervous laughter."[20]

One warm, sunny day in Effingham, Illinois, my companion and I were driving down a rural road with the windows down. Sister Mortensen, who always had a way of making me laugh, was driving the car. Suddenly we heard very loud buzzing sounds. When Sister Mortensen looked at me, I saw two hornets stuck in her long, thick, permed hair. At the look of pure terror I must have given her, she screamed, "What is it? What is it?" I told her she had two yellow jackets in her hair. She yelled at the top of her lungs, "Get them out! Get them out of my hair NOW!" In her panic, her hands were unsteady on the wheel, and the car swerved back and forth on the road. I didn't want to get stung either, so I was screaming, but I was laughing too. Suddenly Sister Mortensen drove off the road into a cornfield that had recently been harvested. She stopped the car and we both jumped out. Sister Mortensen, still in hysterics, flipped her head sideways and ordered, "Get them out! Get them out of my hair, please!" Grabbing a pen from the car, I started jabbing through her hair like a mad woman. Finally, our little troublemakers got untangled and went their separate ways. Then, Sister Mortensen and I doubled over and roared with laughter.

LEARNING TO TRUST IN THE LORD

During my humanitarian trip to the Marshall Islands, there was one day when our dentist and interpreter went to another island to do other dental work. I stayed on the island of Majuro to put sealants on the teeth of all the children in an elementary school. Our interpreter had written several Marshallese phrases on the chalkboard for us to use while he was gone, so all morning I kept saying, "Kabelók lonum." According to the chalkboard, this phrase meant "open your mouth." The kids kept giggling each time they were in my chair, so I thought, "They must think it's so cute that I'm trying to speak Marshallese."

That afternoon, two LDS missionaries arrived at the school to assist us for a few hours and to interpret for us. One Elder was from West Jordan, Utah, and he asked me if I knew what I was saying. I said, "I'm asking them to open their mouths." He laughed and declared, "No, Michelle. You're asking them to open their rear-ends!" It was now 1:30 p.m., so for over half a day I'd been asking children to open their rear-ends. The rest of the week, I could tell which kids I had worked on that first day, because they would giggle and smile at me and say, "Kabelók lonum." Needless to say, no one on our team ever let me forget about this little incident.

Another humorous experience happened to me while on the island of Majuro. After placing sealants on children's teeth and giving brief nutritional seminars, the volunteers decided to go swimming in the island's beautiful lagoon. Up to this point of our trip, I had only waded in the water because I have a funny thing about swimming in natural water. It seems like I always get bitten by something when I do. On a number of occasions I've stepped on jellyfish, and I've received one-too-many weird bug bites. In the Marshall Islands, the rest of the humanitarian workers teased me for not swimming with them, trying to convince me just how clean and safe the water was. Eventually, I caved in and joined them for a swim in the lagoon.

The water was warm, amazingly clear, and indescribably blue. It felt so refreshing. I was in the water no longer than five minutes when my arm hit something or rather was encircled by something! Quickly, I lifted my arm out of the water to see what on earth had a hold of me. It wasn't a snake, a man-eating shark, or even an animal, for that matter. It was a TOILET SEAT! Don't ask me what a toilet seat was doing in the lagoon, because I have no idea. But the rest of the group had swam in the lagoon every evening without seeing so much as a floating candy wrapper! The one time I ventured out in the lagoon, I was attacked by a toilet seat. You can imagine the laughter that followed, and I probably laughed even harder than my friends did.

In President Boyd K. Packer's book *Teach Ye Diligently* he related this story, "When I was attending college, I enrolled in a physiology class. One day during a lecture the professor asked me to sit up on the high table at the front of the room so he could demonstrate the principle of reflexes. He took a little mallet, similar to one a medical doctor would use, and proceeded to tap me on the knee, expecting my leg to jerk noticeably in typical reflex action. However, I held my leg very rigid and flipped my arm in the air when he tapped my knee. The class roared with delight. The professor was not amused."[21]

LEARNING TO TRUST IN THE LORD

CHALLENGE

Take the time to laugh. Think back on your life and write down something funny that happened to you. Share this with a family member or friend, and laugh about it again. Then make a list of what makes you laugh or smile or just plain makes you happy. A few things from my list:

- Babies or children giggling.
- The scene in the movie "Napoleon Dynamite" where Napoleon performs a dance.
- The episode of the "I Love Lucy" show, where Lucille Ball sells a product called "Vitameatavegamin."
- Watching clean and funny movies with family and friends.
- Hiking, snowshoeing, and almost any other activity that combines exercise and nature.
- Spiritually uplifting things like attending the temple, attending church meetings, participating in visiting teaching, reading the scriptures, fasting for others, reading good books, and especially, praying privately.
- Riding the zip-line in Park City, Utah.
- Chocolate and peanut butter—together!
- Traveling to new places, experiencing new cultures, and meeting people from all over the world.

Chapter 8

REMEMBERING LIFE'S LITTLE MIRACLES

I believe we experience little miracles often in our lives, even daily. Some are more obvious than others. They could be anything; from missing a car collision by just a few inches to having good weather for an outdoor wedding reception to an unexpected phone call from a family member or friend. It's important to acknowledge these little miracles and to express gratitude to the Lord for His tender mercies. In President Gordon B. Hinckley's book *Way to Be!*, he stated, "Gratitude creates the most wonderful feeling. It can resolve disputes. It can strengthen friendships. And it can make us better men and women...The habit of thank you is the mark of a cultivated mind."[22]

How many times do we get in the car and pray for safety as we travel, and then arrive at our destination without any "harm or accidents" only to forget to thank the Lord for His protection? We need to recognize the Lord's daily tender mercies in our lives.

While serving in a companionship of three sisters on my mission, I had received more dire news about my mom's cancer and was terribly upset. We tried to call the Elders to come over and give me a blessing of comfort, but they weren't home. All three of us prayed they would come over after their last teaching appointment. Within the hour, we heard a knock on the door. It was our zone leaders, Elder Clarke and Elder Lindhardt. They said that they kept thinking of us sisters and didn't know why, so they had brought us some jam! Well, we knew why, and we were grateful for this direct answer to prayer. I was truly humbled and grateful for the Elders' sensitivity to the Spirit.

For several weeks while serving in my second area on my mission (Burlington, Iowa), I was completely exhausted. It had been weeks since I had slept through the night, because my companion, Sister Lewis, constantly talked, yelled, and walked in her sleep. So one night, Sister Lewis prayed that she would have restful, quiet sleep that night so that I could sleep too. She slept all night without making a sound, and as a result, I slept the entire night all the way through for the first time since we served together. It truly was a miracle.

In Decatur, Illinois, I served with Sister Smart—a great missionary and a little fireball from Sandy, Utah. She was with me when I received the news that my mother was in the ICU suffering from the effects of her cancer. Since the doctors didn't know if mom would make it through the night, it was a torturous time for me. Sister Smart had only been out on her mission for two weeks and felt very homesick. The next morning, we offered a prayer asking Heavenly Father to help us find a family that was ready to hear the gospel that very day. And I prayed that I would have the help I needed to stay on my mission.

After our prayer, Sister Smart and I got in our car, drove to an area in Decatur, and knocked on a few doors. Then we received the impression that this was not where we were supposed to be. We got back into the car and prayed again to know where we should go. Immediately, we both felt strongly that we should go to an area 40 minutes north of town that we had just opened up. We were concerned about putting so many miles on our car, since we were only allotted 1,000 miles a month; however, we both knew without a doubt that this was where the Lord wanted us to go.

As we approached a small city called Maroa, the Holy Ghost prompted us to take the first exit (there were only two), then turn at a specific street, then turn at another street, and then stop in front of a particular house. The Spirit was so strong, we had both felt the impressions. We got out of the car, went to the front door, and read a sign that said, "Every third salesman we shoot, and the second one just left." We knocked anyway, and I must admit being relieved when no one answered. The next door we knocked on was opened by a man who thought Jesus Christ was a spaceman! At this point I wondered, "Lord, where hast Thou taken us?" Feeling a bit discouraged, we walked back onto the street and said a little prayer asking, "Heavenly Father, where are we supposed to be?" Right here! We both received the answer, so we went to the next house—the last one on the street.

After we knocked, a woman answered the door but seemed very hesitant to let us in. She told us she was having surgery in a week and didn't want us to come in. After we talked to her for fifteen minutes on the porch, I received an impression to use a door approach I'd learned from Elder

LEARNING TO TRUST IN THE LORD

Loren C. Dunn of the Seventy when he visited our mission. I said, "Brenda, as representatives of Jesus Christ, we would love to come into your home and leave a blessing on you and your family in the form of a prayer. May we come in and do this?" She smiled and said, "I guess I can't turn down a prayer." As we entered the home we met Brenda's husband, Jimmy, and their nine-year-old son, Jason.

Sister Smart and I knelt and prayed with this humble family. After the prayer, we all had tears in our eyes. Jimmy looked at us and pointed to the *Book of Mormon* in my hand and said, "That's it! That is the book. I want that book!" I said, "Well, sir, here, we are at your home to deliver it to you." Jimmy informed us that he had seen a TV commercial about the *Book of Mormon*, and that just a few days previously he had called the 800 number to order the book. We then taught this family the first discussion and read from the *Book of Mormon* with them. What a sweet and tender first discussion! The family had their share of challenges to overcome, but the Lord blessed them so much.

We later learned that Brenda and Jimmy had been discussing filing for divorce just before we met them, but they changed their minds as they learned the gospel. Four weeks later, the family was baptized. I had never been so specifically guided by the Spirit, and I know the Lord must love this family very much.

Shortly after my mission, my roommate Katrina asked me to be her escort at the Portland Oregon Temple as she received her endowment. While driving on a windy road in southwest Portland on my way to pick her up, I felt a strong impression to slow down. As I slowed the car almost to a stop, the car in front of me lost its hubcap. The hubcap bounced right in front of my car and over it. Had I not slowed down, the flying piece of metal probably would have hit my car, shattered my window and caused an accident. I offered a prayer of thanks and continued on.

Another little miracle occurred as I was taking a biostatistics class in graduate school. This was my "doom" class, and I didn't know how I would get through it. In fact, I felt like the class was being taught in Chinese or some other language I don't speak, since there were so many unfamiliar terms. With my first midterm looming, I started losing sleep over this class. Severe test anxiety makes me literally freeze when taking tests, and I knew this would be the worst of the worst. But the weekend before my midterm, I fasted and prayed that I would be calm and be able to recall all that I had spent many hours studying. Two days later as I took the test, a young woman next to me started to cry as she tried to figure out the problems. Normally, a situation of this sort would send me into a tizzy; however, I remained calm and did extremely well on my exam. All credit for this goes to the Lord Himself!

The miracles continue. A dear friend named Annie was told that her mother, Helen, was dying of pancreatic cancer. Annie has four older, married siblings, and she was saddened that her mother would probably not be there for her wedding. Annie wasn't even dating anyone when her mother was diagnosed, so she had no idea when she would marry. After her diagnosis, Helen and her husband began to pray that Annie would meet someone. Annie was unaware of their prayers. Annie also learned later that someone else's parents were praying for her as well—people she didn't even know.

LEARNING TO TRUST IN THE LORD

Few people diagnosed with pancreatic cancer survive more than six months. Annie's mother, Helen, survived sixteen months after her diagnosis. Helen's cancer continued to take her health as time went by. The great miracle was that Annie met her sweetheart, Jesse, and they were married within that sixteen-month period. Helen felt quite well at the time of the wedding and was able to attend the festivities, and she passed away peacefully six weeks after the wedding. Helen's prayer that she would see all her children married in the temple was answered. Annie's prayer of her mother living long enough to attend her wedding was also answered.

November 15, 2006, is a day I will never forget. I spent a very difficult night by my father's bedside in the ICU at St. Vincent's Hospital in Portland, Oregon. He had been diagnosed six weeks earlier with renal cell carcinoma, so the doctors decided to take out the kidney that was grossly affected. A week after Dad's surgery, he suffered cardiac arrest and complete renal failure, as his remaining kidney couldn't function on its own.

My day had just begun in Utah when I received the news of my father's condition. I immediately drove to the airport to catch the next plane to Portland. When I arrived at the hospital, the physicians advised my siblings and me to have my father's breathing apparatus removed, since there was nothing further that they could do for him. My dad had suffered so much, and after much anguish and prayer, we allowed him to be taken off life support, leaving him to Heavenly Father's care. After being taken off life support, he slipped in and out of consciousness. My siblings and I were all on pins and needles; sixteen years earlier we had taken my mother off life support and she had died within minutes.

A female chaplain from the hospital came in and asked us if we would like to have a harpist play for us. My dad had been so anxious as he came in and out of consciousness. Regular morphine infusions in his IV line kept him free from pain, but his eyes were filled with fear. We decided that the harp was a wonderful idea. An angel of a lady came and played her harp at the foot of Dad's bed for an hour. She played many beautiful songs including *Amazing Grace*.

My sister Mattye and I both cried very hard, but our tears were therapeutic. The veil was very thin, and we knew that there were unseen persons in the room. With the Spirit so strongly manifest, I received a confirmation of the Savior's love for my dad, and a confirmation that He had died for my dad. I also knew the Savior loved me. I'd always known this, but to have another witness was truly beautiful. For the first time since we'd arrived, my dad closed his eyes and really relaxed; he even slept a while. He looked so peaceful following the music, and it calmed and comforted Mattye and me too. I know Heavenly Father and His Son are in the details of our lives, since They are most certainly in the particulars of my life. My father slipped into a comatose state for the next few days, and miraculously, he lived another two and a half months.

Life is a miracle. YOU are a miracle! Many voices in the world want us to believe we are less than who we are. The media tells us what we should wear, watch, eat, and buy to be acceptable. But no matter what we wear or buy or eat or watch, we are all children of God, and His Son died for us collectively and individually. Elder M. Russell Ballard declared:

> "Only as we accept the Atonement in our lives and strive to live the gospel can we meet the challenges of life and find peace, joy, and happiness. I believe that if we could truly understand the Atonement of the Lord Jesus Christ, we would realize how precious is one son or daughter of God...Our Heavenly Father's everlasting purpose for his children is generally achieved by the small and simple things we do for one another. At the heart of the English word Atonement is the word one. If all mankind understood this, there would never be anyone with whom we would not be concerned. We would strive to emulate the Savior and would never be unkind, indifferent, disrespectful, or insensitive to others (or to ourselves).
>
> Sadly in today's world, a person's importance is often judged by the size of the audience before which he or she performs...Yet, in the eyes of the Lord, there may be only one size of audience that is of lasting importance—and that is just one, each one, you and me, and each one of the children of God. The irony of the Atonement is that it is infinite and eternal, yet it is applied individually, one person at a time."[23]

Several years ago, I traveled to the Holy Land, the land of miracles, visiting many cities along the Sea of Galilee. We swam (actually, we floated) in the Dead Sea, hiked along the Judean Desert slopes that overlook the Dead Sea, and hiked to the top of the Masada where 967 Jewish warrior zealots took their lives to defy Herod and the Romans. In addition, we visited several sites where Christ walked and taught in Jerusalem, including the Western Wall, the Dome of the Rock, the pools of Bethesda, the museum of the Dead Sea Scrolls, and Via Delarosa—the path on which Christ carried His cross. We were also privileged to see Yad Vashem, the Holocaust Memorial museum. This served as a very sobering reminder of a terrible period in our world's history. Of all the places we visited, the Garden Tomb and the Garden of Gethsemane were my favorites. Amid the sounds of countless tourists coming and going, I truly felt the Spirit of God witnessing to me of what happened there in the meridian of time.

Another favorite memory of the Holy Land is the time I spent reading the Beatitudes (Matthew 5) by the Sea of Galilee on the hill where Jesus Christ, the Master Teacher, taught the Sermon on the Mount. Since we were there in springtime, beautiful wild poppies in orange, lavender, and red were scattered among the long grass on the hill. The sun shone and a mild breeze came up. It was a surreal, yet unforgettable moment for me, and I can still smell the crisp air when I think about that experience.

The Orson Hyde Memorial, located between the Garden of Gethsemane and the BYU–Jerusalem Center, also gave me an amazing feeling of peace. At this site on October 24, 1841, Apostle Orson Hyde dedicated the land of Israel for the preaching of the gospel. The memorial sits on the Mount of Olives and overlooks the great city of Jerusalem. From my time at the Sea of Galilee; at Tabgha, the site of the miracle of loaves and fishes; and at Shepherd's Field, where the angel appeared to the shepherds declaring the birth of the Savior of the World, I learned to better visualize the life and character of Jesus Christ.

Every one of us witnesses little miracles every day, and as we recognize them, it's vital to express our gratitude to Heavenly Father. Giving thanks empowers us to receive more of the Lord's abundance in our lives. I believe our gratitude also empowers us to trust in the Lord more fully. As President Hinckley noted, "Gratitude creates the most wonderful feeling."[24]

CHALLENGE

Think back in your life to times when the Lord has revealed to you who you really are. Write these experiences in your journal and share them, if you feel comfortable, with your family either now or later in life. In addition, seek opportunities to help others—your child, a niece, a nephew, or another young person—know who he or she really is.

Chapter 9

GOD BLESS AMERICA

We are so blessed to live in a land where we enjoy so many freedoms. I'm grateful for our freedom of religion, freedom of the press, freedom of speech, freedom to be educated, freedom to vote, and countless other freedoms. Joseph Smith called the U.S. Constitution a "Heavenly Banner."

It has been my privilege to see many historical sites in the United States. I have visited the Statue of Liberty, Independence Hall, Washington D.C., Plymouth Rock, Pearl Harbor, and Gettysburg. One cannot travel to these places without feeling a deep appreciation for our country and the men and women that have sacrificed their lives for our freedom. As I visit each site, I try to buy a book that tells the history—even just an educational children's book with photographs or illustrations. My collection includes books about the Statue of Liberty, Gettysburg, the Mayflower, a memoir of a child living in Honolulu during Pearl Harbor, and a book about the Constitution of the United States. I always feel such a deep sense of gratitude and love for my country when I read these inspiring books.

LEARNING TO TRUST IN THE LORD

Being an American is a great blessing, especially as a woman. In many countries, women have no voice at all, no opportunities. On the streets of Ho Chi Minh City, Vietnam, a three-year-old girl tried to sell me a package of gum and some cigarettes. What is the future for that girl? I lost sleep over that little girl! Here in America, we women can own land, vote, and follow our dreams. And we can receive an education.

Recently, I read a book called *My Forbidden Face*, a memoir of a young woman living under Taliban rule in Afghanistan. The author, who calls herself only "Latifa," writes how women were mostly confined to their homes, and when they did go outside, they were required by law to wear a burka, a veil that covers the face and hair. And according to Latifa, Afghani women suffered many atrocities. For example, Latifa writes of a teenage girl who had her fingers chopped off because she wore fingernail polish. Latifa watched her mother, a physician, assist women in childbirth as well as tend to their other medical needs, all done in secret in their homes. Men were not allowed to deliver babies, yet women were prevented by law from openly practicing medicine. Consequently, women would go through labor and childbirth without medical assistance or help, and many women and infants died as a result. Latifa's mother would have been imprisoned and possibly tortured or executed if she were caught practicing medicine, but out of her own humanity she did it anyway.

When the Taliban took over the Afghani government, all opportunities for females—including education—became illegal. For over a year Latifa felt powerless. Finally, with great determination, she decided to follow her mother's incredible courage, starting a small school in her home. Although this was illegal, Latifa couldn't stand the thought of the young girls in her apartment complex not learning how to read. This continued for several years, during which time Latifa miraculously gained access to the books her students needed. To take a stand for something good is one thing, but to do so when you could be tortured or executed for it is another thing entirely.

I am grateful for our local libraries where I am free to check out a book—any book I want—and to read it. Although this seems like a simple thing, think how often we take even our local libraries for granted. In Afghanistan and in many other countries, books were often burned, and this is still the case in some countries.

Elder Holland said, "Education is to help us learn who we really are and discover what God expects us to do. One thing he expects us to remember is that we are heirs of a gospel dispensation that had among its earliest commandments that challenge to 'seek...diligently and teach one another words of wisdom; yea, seek...out of the best of books...learning, even by study and also by faith.' God's glory is intelligence, and it is to be our glory as well."[25]

Another favorite story is of an African American woman named Susie King Taylor. While living in slavery, young Susie secretly learned how to read. She escaped as a teenager and worked as a laundress, then later a nurse, a cook, and a teacher. Susie bravely assisted the Union cause during the Civil War, and her contributions made a difference.[26]

In the *Doctrine and Covenants* and the *Book of Mormon*, we learn that the land of America—which includes North, Central, and South America—was chosen by God for fulfillment of His purposes. As the Jaredites prepared to journey to the promised land, the Lord told the brother of Jared, "And there will I meet thee, and I will go before thee into a land which is choice above all the lands of the earth. And there will I bless thee and thy seed, and raise up unto me of thy seed, and of the seed of thy brother, and they who shall go with thee, a great nation. And there shall be none greater than the nation which I will raise up unto me of thy seed, upon all the face of the earth" (Ether 1:42–43).

Our forefathers fought to establish the U.S. Constitution and Declaration of Independence, and without the freedom of religion established thereby, the true Church could not have been restored to the earth. The Lord prepared this land for the Restoration of the fullness of the gospel. What a tremendous blessing is our freedom of religion—our freedom to worship how, when, and where we want according to the dictates of our own consciences. President George Albert Smith testified:

> "In no other nation under heaven could the Church have been organized and gone forward as we have in this nation. The founding of the United States was not an accident. Our Heavenly Father knew what would be needed, and so he paved the way to give us the Constitution. It came under the influence of prayer, and he guided those who framed that wonderful document. God watched over those who settled the land of America. [1 Nephi 13: 12-19] refers to Christopher Columbus and the Pilgrim fathers. It was the Lord that inspired that little band of people who crossed the mighty ocean and landed at Plymouth

Rock, because they desired to worship him according to the dictates of their own conscience. He watched over them and safeguarded their descendants and those who followed them to America, and in due time, there came an opportunity to establish liberty such as humankind had not known before."[27]

What a great blessing it is to live in America and to enjoy the many freedoms and privileges that we do. Let us remember that freedom is not free! Our freedom was won by the thousands of men and women who have given their lives in defense of our country. When I visited places such as Vietnam, Pearl Harbor, Concord, Gettysburg, and Ground Zero in New York, I experienced an overwhelming sense of gratitude for the sacrifices made that we may live in freedom. I am also grateful that our coinage professes our belief in a Higher Power with the words *In God We Trust*.

CHALLENGE

I challenge you to read a book about American history. Pick a city or historical site in the United States such as Gettysburg, Washington D.C., or Pearl Harbor, then go to your local library and check out a book that describes the historical events that took place there. Also, further your education in any way you can. If you have been thinking about going back to school, stop thinking about it and do it! As Abraham Lincoln remarked, "I don't think much of a man who is not wiser today than he was yesterday."[28]

Chapter 10

WOMEN WHO HAVE GONE BEFORE US

Many elect women have set extraordinary examples of patterning their lives after the Savior's life. These amazing women from both ancient and modern times exemplify true faith and devotion to God.

Although she's not in the scriptures and wasn't a very religious person, there couldn't be a more Christ-like person than my own mother. I hope you'll indulge me in a few more brief stories about her. During my childhood, my mother taught me how to be a good friend. When I was in the third grade, we had just moved from Reno, Nevada to Toppenish, Washington. At my new school, many of the kids made fun of a particular girl because she had a very large, red birthmark. In fact, the birthmark covered about 60 percent of her body. I remember seeing the hurt look on her face when my classmates said disparaging things to her.

When I told my mother about my classmate with the birthmark, she sat me down and discussed with me the need to be especially kind to this girl and told me how lonely it must be for her. My mother also specifically asked me to never join in ridiculing the girl. Although this girl and I never became close friends, I tried to be kind to her and in so doing learned a powerful lesson.

The same year, I met a girl named Lynn, who was a member of my community swim team. Lynn had a deformed hand and arm, and kids mocked her for being "different." Once again, my mother talked with me privately about being kind and extending a hand of friendship to Lynn. One day I called Lynn on the phone to talk about an upcoming swim meet and she invited me to swim and sleep over at her house. Because of my mother's counsel, I decided I didn't care what others might say about me if I spent time with Lynn. In fact, Lynn became one of my most cherished friends during our brief two years in Washington.

As far as I know, my mother never said a bad word about anyone. On one occasion during high school, I was talking on the phone with a friend about another girl and my mother entered the room. When she overheard part of my conversation, she signaled me to hang up and gave me a "talking to." She told me not to speak negatively of anyone, and she also counseled me to keep confidences with friends. My mother said on several occasions, "What you say about others somehow always comes back to you, so make sure it's something you would say if they were present." Those are great words to live by.

My mother always embraced my friends and was so generous to them. Once when a friend of mine was struggling with a very difficult circumstance, my mother sat down and took the time to listen to her, refraining from judgment and carefully counseling her.

LEARNING TO TRUST IN THE LORD

Throughout my life I watched my mother, year after year, handwrite almost one hundred Christmas cards to friends she had kept in touch with over the years. She regularly corresponded with Norma, her best friend from childhood. While in the first grade, my mother had raised her hand to go to the restroom and when the teacher refused to call on her, she wet her pants. Norma sat behind my mother and felt bad about what happened, so she befriended my mother. After that, Norma and my mother were inseparable friends, and this lasted throughout all their school years. Even after they each got married and lived in different states, they always stayed in touch. After my mother passed away from ovarian cancer, I flew to Arizona where Norma lived with her husband and interviewed her about her friendship with my mother. She shared many wonderful stories of her and my mother's growing-up years and how they truly were kindred spirit friends.

As stated previously, my mother was diagnosed with terminal cancer when I had only been in the mission field for two months. Because of the cancer, my mother's financial burden was heavy, but she insisted on sending money to my bishop every month to help pay for my mission. My mother taught me the importance of keeping my word, as she kept her promise to write to me every week on my mission. Even when she was seriously ill and in the hospital, she would ask the nurse for a pen and paper so she could write to her missionary daughter. I now have these letters in chronological order; they are one of my most cherished possessions.

As long as I can remember, whether it was at her work or in the neighborhood, my mother always went out of her way to befriend people. On several occasions, she stayed after work to listen to someone talk about his or her problems. When my parents separated, it was a grueling time for my mother. She met a friend at work named Nancy, whom she had been helping through some difficult things. Now Nancy was there for my mother, and Nancy and her husband were very kind to her. From my mother I learned the importance of being there for friends during their difficult times, as well as the importance of letting our friends be there for us. Even the Savior, during the most difficult time of His life, needed His friends. In the New Testament, we read that He asked Peter, James, and John to wait outside the Garden of Gethsemane while He took upon Himself the sins of the world. I'm grateful for a mother who lived her life with an extraordinary example of love and friendship.

My mother, an incredibly selfless person, sacrificed so much for me throughout her life. After my parents separated and divorced, my mother worked relentless hours to provide the necessities of life. This was such a dark and difficult time for all of us, and I'm certain it was hardest on my mother. But throughout this time and until the day she died, my mother was her children's greatest cheerleader; she believed in us and told us we could do anything we wanted.

Another extraordinary woman is Frances Johnson Monson, the wife of our prophet, President Thomas S. Monson. Although comparatively little has been written about her to date, she is an elect lady in every way. Sister Monson stated, "From the day of our marriage, Tom has served in leadership positions. Some have asked how a new bride adjusts to that, but it has never been a sacrifice to see my husband doing the Lord's work…It has blessed me, and it has blessed our children. He always knew that if it was for the Church, I expected him to do what he had to do."[29]

And speaking of his dear Frances, President Monson said, "In 59 years of marriage I have never known Frances to complain once of my church responsibilities. In those 59 years I have been gone many days and many nights, and I have rarely been able to sit with her in the congregation. But there is no one like her—absolutely no one. She is in every way supportive and is a woman of quiet and profoundly powerful faith."[30]

We have much to learn from Sister Monson. If you are married, do you sustain your spouse in his or her church callings? I'm grateful for Sister Monson's quiet, yet influential example of faith.

At BYU Women's Conference in 1999, Sister Ruth Faust said of Sister Frances Monson, "She has a quiet dignity about her and she is a woman of great integrity."[31] During this panel discussion of the First Presidency's wives and their daughters, Sister Monson was asked by her daughter Ann to share one of her favorite experiences with President Monson.

Sister Monson named their mission together in Toronto, Canada, where President Monson served as mission president. Sister Monson also told of a trip to Germany with her husband after the wall had been torn down. She said, "One of the most interesting experiences that I can remember was going to Germany after the wall went down. I remember seeing that on television, I imagine most of you did, they were tearing down the wall. I said to my husband, 'Oh, I would love to be there when they were tearing down the wall.' This was because my husband had worked with the

East German Saints for about 20 years, and he loved them. He had many opportunities in his life working with the German people."[32]

Sister Monson then shared the miracle that allowed President Monson and her to make that trip to Germany:

> "My husband awakened one night; the church was having a big conference with the German saints and he told her he needed to go to that meeting. I said, "President Benson is in critical condition in the hospital, there is no way you can leave." He said, "I just have to go." The next morning, President Hinckley talked to him and said, "I think we should go to the hospital, and give President Benson a blessing...so they did. He wasn't expected to live. President Hinckley and my husband gave him that blessing and promised him that he would live and get better...his family was amazed. The next day, he was moved out of intensive care, then eventually home to his apartment. With nursing care, he lived about two to three years after that blessing.
>
> We went to that meeting in Germany with the saints; it was the most spiritual and fantastic meeting I have ever attended. To see families reunited again after 40 years of being separated. It was something you could never ever realize the inspiration that came to that meeting and to be with those people...The Lord blessed us, He blessed President Benson and all those wonderful people. That was one of my most wonderful experiences I have had and I loved that very much. And I love to travel with him."[33]

Sister Monson closed her thoughts from the panel discussion with her testimony, "I know the church is true. I've been blessed; I think I've been brought back to life literally a couple times because of blessings and the Lord's inspiration in helping me. I love my association with these sisters [Sister Marjorie Hinckley and Sister Ruth Faust] and all the general authorities and their wives. And meeting with people throughout the world—they are wonderful."[34]

I had my own personal experience with President and Sister Monson. Several years ago, I attended a work party where our entire dental office went boating and rode wave runners. My boss' family cabin was located across the street from the Monson's cabin in one of the canyons in northern Utah. As we pulled up to my boss' cabin, we had just returned from the lake, so we were sunburned and our hair was a mess. Across the street, President Monson was working in the front yard of his cabin, and he was wearing jeans! (It's not often that you see a prophet wearing jeans, although I'm certain they do. We're just so used to seeing them in suits.)

We walked across the street and after greetings were exchanged, I said to President Monson, "I know it's July and this is your month off, but could we get a quick picture with you?" He smiled and said, "Why sure!" As we all gathered around President Monson for the photograph, Frances peeked her head out the front door and said something like, "Tom, honey, you'd better comb your hair." We all smiled to see her looking out for her husband, even in the little things. Frances Monson is in my eyes a truly elect lady.

One of my favorite heroes from Church history is Lucy Mack Smith, the mother of the Prophet Joseph Smith.

Like Nephi of old, she was born of goodly parents. In fact, one of the last admonitions Lucy Mack Smith received from her mother before her passing was, "I beseech you to continue faithful in the service of God to the end of your days, that I may have the pleasure of embracing you in another and fairer world above."[35]

I believe firmly that Lucy Mack Smith was commissioned by the Lord to bear and raise the great Prophet of the Restoration. Before and after the First Vision, Lucy sought inspiration from God and prayed to know the true gospel. In 1804—a year before Joseph Jr. was born—Lucy had been offended in a family dispute between her husband, Joseph, and his brother, Jesse. In her own words:

> "I retired to a grove not far distant, where I prayed to the Lord in behalf of my husband—that the true gospel might be presented to him and that his heart might be softened so as to receive it, or, that he might become more religiously inclined. After praying some time in this manner, I returned to the house much depressed in spirit, which state of feeling continued until I retired to my bed. I soon fell asleep and had the following dream: I thought that I stood in a large and beautiful meadow, which lay a short distance from the house in which we lived, and that everything around me wore an aspect of peculiar pleasantness. The first thing that attracted my special attention in this magnificent meadow, was a very pure and clear stream of water, which ran through the midst of it; and as I traced this stream, I discovered two trees standing upon its

margin, both of which were very beautiful, they were well proportioned, and towered with majestic beauty to a great height. Their branches, which added to their symmetry and glory, commenced near the top, and spread themselves in luxurious grandeur around. I gazed upon them with wonder and admiration; and after beholding them a short time, I saw one of them was surrounded with a bright belt, that shone like burnished gold, but far more brilliantly. Presently, a gentle breeze passed by, and the tree encircled with this golden zone, bent gracefully before the wind, and waved its beautiful branches in the light air. As the wind increased, this tree assumed the most lively and animated appearance, and seemed to express in its motions the utmost joy and happiness. If it had been an intelligent creature, it could not have conveyed, by the power of language, the idea of joy and gratitude so perfectly as it did; and even the stream that rolled beneath it, shared, apparently, every sensation felt by the tree, for, as the branches danced over the stream, it would swell gently, then recede again with a motion as soft as the breathing of an infant, but as lively as the dancing of a sunbeam. The belt also partook of the same influence, and, as it moved in unison with the motion of the stream and of the tree, it increased continually in refulgence and magnitude, until it became exceedingly glorious.

    I turned my eyes upon its fellow, which stood opposite; but it was not surrounded with the belt of light as former, and it stood erect and fixed as a pillar of marble. No matter how strong the wind blew over it; not a leaf was stirred, not a bough was bent; but obstinately stiff it stood, scorning alike the zephyr's breath, or the power of the mighty storm.

I wondered at what I saw, and said in my heart, what can be the meaning of all this? And the interpretation given me was, that these personated my husband and his oldest brother, Jesse Smith; that the stubborn and unyielding tree was like Jesse; that the other, more pliant and flexible, was like Joseph, my husband; that the breath of heaven, which passed over them, was the pure and undefiled gospel of the Son of God, which gospel Jesse would always resist, but which Joseph, when he was more advance in life, would hear and receive with his whole heart, and rejoice therein; and unto him would be added intelligence, happiness, glory, and everlasting life."[36]

What a powerful dream! Is there any question that Lucy Mack Smith was one of the noble and great ones mentioned in Abraham, and prepared to come to this earth to raise and teach the Prophet of the Restoration?

Elder M. Russell Ballard said of Lucy Mack Smith, "She gave continual encouragement, support, and strength to her son, Joseph the Prophet. His mother was the first person with whom young Joseph shared some of his momentous experiences of the Sacred Grove."[37]

Lucy Mack Smith was an extraordinary woman who patterned her life after the Savior's life and sacrificed much for the kingdom of God. How grateful we should be for her example, her faithfulness, and all she did to help bring about the restoration of Jesus Christ's true church.

In addition to Lucy Mack Smith, there is a plethora of noble women in the scriptures and Church history, including Mary, Emma Smith, Eve, Esther, Ruth, Abish, to name just a few. I'm grateful for the part each faithful woman has taken in accomplishing the Lord's work. Mary, the mother of Jesus Christ is another one of my heroes. We can learn much from Mary's life, especially the importance of being pure and virtuous that we might help fulfill God's purposes. As we read in Alma 7:10, Mary was "a virgin, a precious and chosen vessel." Emma Smith, the Prophet Joseph's wife, was commanded by the Lord to "Walk in the paths of virtue before me, I will preserve thy life, and thou shalt receive an inheritance in Zion" (D&C 25:2). The counsel applies to all of us as well. As we cleave to virtue, we are promised that the Holy Ghost will guide us.

The second lesson we can learn from Mary is the importance of pondering. Luke 2:19 reads, "But Mary kept all these things, and pondered them in her heart." Many times, I've received personal promptings while reading and pondering the scriptures, and I'm certain you have as well. As we ponder the things of God in our lives, we allow the Holy Ghost to teach us our divine roles here on earth. Elder Marion D. Hanks explained, "Our minds also need to be prepared to pray. Through search and study we can begin to learn what we need to know. And we must think—actively, consciously, quietly, reflectively, honestly, deeply think. Then we can in good conscience come to the Lord to seek wisdom, comfort, strength, grace or courage."[38] Notice that Elder Hanks says we should seek heavenly help only after we think on and ponder the things of God. I believe this is because only then are we prepared to receive Heavenly Father's counsel.

Mary, the mother of Jesus, was a woman of God and not of the world. While serving as Young Women general president, Margaret D. Nadauld stated, "Women of God can never be like women of the world. The world has enough women who are tough; we need women who are tender. There are enough women who are coarse; we need women who are kind. There are enough women who are rude; we need women who are refined. We have enough women of fame and fortune; we need more women of faith. We have enough greed; we need more goodness. We have enough vanity; we need more virtue. We have enough popularity; we need more purity."[39]

I am grateful for extraordinary women who have gone before me and who are still with us, who are a prevailing influence for good in our lives. May we strive to be like them and pattern our lives after the Savior's life.

CHALLENGE

Handwrite and mail a letter to an exemplary woman in your life: your mother, grandmother, sister, aunt, Young Women leader, Relief Society leader, etc. After I taught Relief Society one Sunday, I didn't feel that my lesson had gone very well. But afterwards, as I gathered my lesson materials, I found a brief note on the table that said, "Michelle, and to think I wasn't going to come today! Thank you for your beautiful lesson." This letter is now taped in my journal.

Chapter 11

TRUST IN THE LORD

Talking and writing about completely trusting in the Lord is so much easier than actually doing it. So many times when we face our Red Seas of life, we take out that backpack with our scuba gear, just in case—or at least I do. Submitting our will to the Lord's is the only way to achieve the happiness that we desire and that He has designed for us. As Elder Neal A. Maxwell declared, "It is only by yielding to God that we can begin to realize His will for us. And if we truly trust God, why not yield to His loving omniscience? After all, He knows us and our possibilities much better than we do."[40]

While I was at the Missionary Training Center, Ed J. Pinegar presided over the missionaries. Every morning, President Pinegar would talk to us over the intercom. He always started out saying, "Good morning, my missionaries. I love you." Then he would say, "I love you" in several different languages. One morning, he added, "Heavenly Father loves it when we laugh. It's okay to laugh, and you should laugh." I have never forgotten this message.

In the April 2006 General Priesthood Session of General Conference, President Dieter F. Uchtdorf stated:

> "We don't always know the details of our future. We do not know what lies ahead. We live in a time of uncertainty. We are surrounded by challenges on all sides. Occasionally discouragement may sneak into our day; frustration may invite itself into our thinking; doubt might enter about the value of our work. In these dark moments Satan whispers in our ears that we will never be able to succeed, that the price isn't worth the effort, and that our small part will never make a difference. He, the father of all lies, will try to prevent us from seeing the end from the beginning. Fortunately, you…are taught by prophets, seers, and revelators of our day. The First Presidency said, "We have great confidence in you. You are choice spirits…Your Heavenly Father wants your life to be joyful and to lead you back into his presence."[41]

I am approaching my 40th year and I have not yet had the privilege of marriage. There are many amazing single Latter-Day Saint women, and I sometimes feel like the single men have a Nordstrom-caliber selection of women to choose from. I know the Lord has a plan for me, but sometimes trusting in His timing takes a bit more faith. A few years ago, I attended a friend's temple wedding; she was 38-years-old and had never been married. The sealer said to her and her fiancé, "You have come this far with much patience; patience is a form of long-suffering."

LEARNING TO TRUST IN THE LORD

Whether you are waiting for marriage, waiting to get pregnant and bear children, waiting for educational or occupational opportunities—or waiting to fulfill any other righteous goal—trusting in the Lord's timing and purposes is vital. As we read in D&C 98:1–3:

> Verily I say unto you my friends; fear not, let your hearts be comforted; yea, rejoice evermore, and in everything give thanks;
> Waiting patiently on the Lord, for your prayers have entered into the ears of the Lord of Sabaoth, and are recorded with this seal and testament—the Lord hath sworn and decreed that they shall be granted.
> Therefore, he giveth this promise unto you, with an immutable covenant that they shall be fulfilled; and all things wherewith you have been afflicted shall work together for your good and to my name's glory, saith the Lord.

Another scripture that brings comfort is found in the *Book of Mormon,* "Do ye not remember the things which the Lord hath said? If ye will not harden your hearts, and ask me in faith, believing that ye shall receive, with diligence in keeping the commandments, surely these things shall be made known unto you" (1 Nephi 15:11).

After graduating from school, while I worked part-time as a dental hygienist, I searched for a full-time job where I could use my new degree. I received a few job offers, but they just didn't feel right. In other positions that I interviewed for it would come down to just me and one other interviewee.

The job would always be offered to the other candidate. How frustrating! But the Lord was definitely looking out for me. Around this same time was when my father was diagnosed with cancer, and due to my light schedule at the dental office, I was able to go to Portland to see him. In fact, I traveled there three times in three months to spend time with my father and to be there when he passed away. If I had started a new job, I wouldn't have had the flexibility to leave so often. The Lord also knew that I would need emotional support from my coworkers—who had become close friends of mine—to help me through that time. How grateful I was for the Lord's tender mercies in making sure I didn't have a new full-time job at that particular time.

Staying close to the Lord and saturating ourselves with His Spirit will empower us to trust Him—and to trust in His timing! As we continue to learn of Him, we will start to know His character, and we will know and understand His omnipotence. The Lord truly is all-powerful and all loving.

I would like to share with you a few suggestions for growing closer to Heavenly Father and to the Savior. While some of these may seem like "Sunday School answers," we need to hear them repeatedly, since most of us are still guilty of sins of omission. (Ouch! I know; but please keep reading.) Although there are many things we can do to come to know the character of the Lord, I will talk about just four.

One—Attend the Temple

Recently, after being called to serve in my singles' ward Relief Society presidency, we met with the Relief Society

General Board members for a training meeting just before General Conference. Each sister who attended the meeting received a copy of the booklet *Preparing to Enter the Holy Temple,* written by Boyd K. Packer. The sister conducting the training challenged us to read the booklet several times, even if we were already endowed. As I did the requested reading, I knew I was learning pure doctrine as taught by an apostle of Jesus Christ. And when I have attended the temple since reading the booklet, I have been more open to learning the truths taught there.

The Savior taught that His Father's house, the temple, was a place of learning. When the twelve-year-old Jesus was found missing from the caravan traveling from Jerusalem to Galilee, Joseph and Mary returned and located Him in the temple. The twelve-year-old Jesus sat answering the questions of the priests, who were doctors of the law themselves—and He had been there for three days (JST Luke 2:46).

Throughout the scriptures, particularly the *Doctrine & Covenants* and the book of *Revelation,* we read of the great calamities that will befall the earth in the last days, including war, famine, plagues, earthquakes, great storms, and many other terrible things. But we have also received the assurance found in D&C 87:8, "Wherefore, stand ye in holy places, and be not moved, until the day of the Lord come; for behold it cometh quickly, saith the Lord."

Elder Neal A. Maxwell remarked, "Temples are designed not only to endow and to seal us but also to refine us."[42] I'm so grateful for temples, where we can receive the Lord's refining.

The two years I attended dental hygiene school, I was extremely busy. When I started school, I decided to attend the temple every month so I could stay spiritually grounded. I never missed a month during those two years, and my temple attendance brought such peace to my life. During this time, I had three great roommates; as a result, our household was always busy. Only at the temple could I really "be still" and reflect on God's plan for me.

Two—Study the Scriptures

If we want to know the Lord, we must search the scriptures, where we find the Lord's own words as well as the words of His prophets. Bruce R. McConkie remarked, "I think that people who study the scriptures get a dimension to their life that nobody else gets and that can't be gained in any way except by studying the scriptures. There's an increase in faith and a desire to do what's right and a feeling of inspiration and understanding that comes to people who study the gospel—meaning particularly the Standard Works—and who ponder the principles, that can't come in any other way."[43]

One of the greatest ways to learn about the Savior is by reading the *Book of Mormon*. My favorite thing to do as a missionary was to read the *Book of Mormon* out loud with our investigators, because this always invited the Spirit of the Lord into the room. We all remember when President Gordon B. Hinckley challenged the members of the Church to read the *Book of Mormon* by the end of that year (*Ensign*, August 2006). And we all heard many members' wonderful experiences of following this inspired counsel, and how there was an extra measure of the Spirit in their homes as a result of reading or rereading the *Book of Mormon*. As I followed

LEARNING TO TRUST IN THE LORD

President Hinckley's counsel, it was another witness of the fact that the Lord is bound when we do what He says. Have you noticed that the times you feel the farthest from the Lord are when you aren't consistent with your scripture studying?

Elder Russell M. Nelson testified, "Do you want to get rid of a bad habit? Do you want to improve relationships in your family? Do you want to increase your spiritual capacity? Read the *Book of Mormon!* It will bring you closer to the Lord and His loving power. He who fed a multitude with five loaves and two fishes—He who helped the blind to see and the lame to walk—can also bless you! He has promised that those who live by the precepts of this book shall receive a crown of eternal life...*The Book of Mormon* is true!"[44]

One experience with the *Book of Mormon* I will always treasure happened on my mission. Each year around Thanksgiving, our mission had a "week of truth," during which every missionary read the entire *Book of Mormon*. This particular week, my companion and I had numerous teaching appointments and before we knew it, we had one day left to read the entire book! On the night we realized this, the Elders called to get our weekly report. After asking for the usual statistics—how many contacts we'd made, how many discussions we'd taught, etc.—they asked if we were participating in the "week of truth." My companion, who had answered the phone, looked at me and smiled. Then with a look of serious conviction on her face, she said, "Yes, Elder, we'll be done by tomorrow." I remember thinking that she must be mental! When she hung up the phone, we decided to start reading the *Book of Mormon* immediately. We read the entire book out loud together and read straight through the night until sometime the next day. It was an amazing experience! I will never forget how the Spirit accompanied us that night. Elder Dallin H. Oaks taught:

> "Scripture reading may...lead to current revelation on whatever [subject] the Lord wishes to communicate to the reader at that time. We do not overstate the point when we say that the scriptures can be a Urim and Thummim to assist each of us to receive personal revelation.
> Because we believe that scripture reading can help us receive revelation, we are encouraged to read the scriptures again and again. By this means, we obtain access to what our Heavenly Father would have us know and do in our personal lives today. That is one reason Latter-day Saints believe in daily scripture study."[45]

Undoubtedly, you want to learn the Lord's will for your life—what He would have you know and do. I know that Elder Oak's counsel is true, that as we study scriptures they can be as our own Urim and Thummim through which we can receive personal revelation.

Three—Pray

Personal prayer is crucial in cultivating a relationship with Heavenly Father and in learning of His character. I'm so grateful that God—an omnipotent, perfect Being who knows and loves each of us individually—allows, and in fact commands us, to communicate with Him. Fasting and prayer together is a powerful way to call upon the power of the Holy Ghost.

LEARNING TO TRUST IN THE LORD

After the attacks on America on September 11, 2001, most of the country was united in prayer. So many lives were lost, and others were thrown into chaos. You probably got on your knees to pray for those directly affected by this tragedy, and perhaps you even knew someone who was injured or killed in the attacks. On that day, terrorists threatened both our physical safety and our freedom, but there is a far more serious threat to our eternal well-being.

Satan and his associates are attacking more than just our freedom—they are attempting to destroy our moral agency. And this full-blown spiritual attack rages every single day, never relenting or sleeping. Are we pleading on our knees for the power to resist temptation, for the spirit of discernment? Are we praying for, as Elder David A. Bednar called it, "the supernal companionship of the Holy Ghost?"[46] Are we praying for the welfare of those souls who don't know the Lord? Whether praying individually, with family or friends, in church meetings, or united as a nation, what a great blessing it is to join our faith and to offer humble words to our Heavenly Father.

The Prophet Joseph Smith remarked, "It is the privilege of the children of God to come to God and get revelation...God is not a respecter of persons, we all have the same privilege." He also said, and I love this quote, "We believe that we have a right to revelations, visions, and dreams from God, our Heavenly Father, and light and intelligence, through the gift of the Holy Ghost, in the name of Jesus Christ, on all subjects pertaining to our spiritual welfare; if it so be that we keep his commandments, so as to render ourselves worthy in his sight."[47] I am eternally grateful for prayer.

Four—Repent and Forgive

The fourth suggestion for learning about the character of God is to honestly repent of our sins and to sincerely forgive others. In fact, both daily repentance and daily forgiveness are essential in coming closer to the Lord. President George Albert Smith declared, "Today I am thinking of the need not only of prayer, not only of faith—the world is teaching that, too—but I am thinking of the need, the sublime need… of repentance from the things of the world and the turning away from the temptations that afflict mankind."[48]

The Savior's Atonement is the greatest gift ever offered, and its most sublime blessings are available to every contrite soul. When my friend Shelly was a little girl, she would regularly visit a convenience store near her house, and occasionally she would take a little piece of candy without paying. As the years went on and she became more spiritually mature, she thought about what she had done and decided to talk to the store owner, who was also a family friend. She confessed to him that she had stolen candy from his store as a child, to which he replied, "I know." A bit startled, Shelly asked why he had never called her on it. He explained, "I knew your heart, and I knew one day you would come back to me and apologize."

This is exactly how Heavenly Father is with us. He knows us regardless of what we have done—He knows our hearts. And even though He is well aware of our weaknesses and our sins, His arms are always open wide to receive us, and His hands are stretched out still. As the Hymn says, "He reaches our reaching…Constant He is and kind, Love with-out end."[49]

LEARNING TO TRUST IN THE LORD

A powerful example of the Lord's forgiveness and grace is found in the story of John Newton. Newton was a slave trader in the mid 1700s. On his watch, over twenty thousand African slaves—men, women, and children—died due to the inhumane conditions on the ships that transported them to America. One night in March 1748, Newton's ship *The Greyhound* almost sank during a furious Atlantic storm. As the storm raged, Newton realized the enormity of his sins and pleaded with God to forgive him, promising that if God would spare his life, he would spend it trying to make amends for his wrongdoings.

Keeping his promise, Newton devoted his life to the ministry and to working for the abolition of slavery. He was a mentor to Wilbur Wilberforce, a member of the British Parliament whose efforts contributed to the abolishment of the slave trade throughout the British Empire. John Newton never ceased to stand in awe of God's work in his life. His life is a great story of a man's triumph over his demons, of true repentance, and of making great retribution for one's sins.[50] It was Newton who wrote the words to one of our most beloved Hymns; *Amazing Grace,* "Amazing Grace, how sweet the sound that saved a wretch like me. I once was lost, but now I'm found, was blind, but now I see!"

In March 1805, the elderly John Newton wrote in his diary, "Not well able to write, but I endeavor to observe the return of this day with humiliation, prayer and praise. Only God's amazing grace could and would take a rude, profane, slave-trading sailor and transform him into a child of God."[51]

Our Father in Heaven beckons us to approach Him with a repentant heart and in an attitude of forgiveness toward others.

As we let go of anger and learn to forgive others, we open ourselves to love in our life. In a previous chapter of this book, I shared the story of my friend Lisa, whose father was shot and killed by one of his patients. Lisa's experience is a perfect example of forgiveness in extremely difficult circumstances.

On the other hand, an acquaintance of mine hasn't spoken to her mother for almost 20 years. While I don't know the circumstances and don't seek to judge her or her mother, the situation seems tragic, no matter the reasons for the silence. Until we forgive those who have hurt us, we carry festering wounds in our souls that permit us from truly being whole in other relationships. That said, in situations where there have been severe offenses, a person may need professional counseling to help process difficult emotions and to move toward with forgiveness and peace.

From the Redeemer of the world, we learn the greatest lesson of forgiveness. On the cross, He said, "Father, forgive them for they know not what they do" (Luke 23:34). Elder Jeffrey R. Holland stated, "Surely the reason Christ said "Father, forgive them" was because even in the weakened and terribly trying hour he faced, he knew that this was the message he had come through all eternity to deliver…the entire plan of salvation… would have been lost had he forgotten that not *in spite of* injustice and brutality and unkindness and disobedience but precisely *because* of them had he come to extend forgiveness to the family of man…It is the quintessential moment of his ministry, and as perfect in its example as it was difficult to endure."[52]

Another striking example of forgiveness comes from Corrie ten Boom. After the war ended, this Holocaust survivor shared with groups of all faiths her testimony of the Savior's peace and of the miracle of repentance. Here is her amazing account of one such experience:

"It was at a church service in Munich that I saw him, the former S.S. man who had stood guard at the shower room door in the processing center at Ravensbruck. He was the first of our actual jailers that I had seen since that time. And suddenly it was all there—the roomful of mocking men, the heaps of clothing, Betsie's pain-blanched face.

He came up to me as the church was emptying, beaming and bowing. "How grateful I am for your message, Fraulein," he said. "To think that, as you say, He has washed my sins away!" His hand was thrust out to shake mine. And I, who had preached so often to the people in Bloemendaal the need to forgive, kept my hand at my side.

Even as the angry, vengeful thoughts boiled through me, I saw the sin of them. Jesus Christ had died for this man; was I going to ask for more? Lord Jesus, I prayed, forgive me and help me to forgive him.

I tried to smile; I struggled to raise my hand. I could not. I felt nothing, not the slightest spark of warmth or charity. And so again I breathed a silent prayer. Jesus, I cannot forgive him. Give me Your forgiveness.

As I took his hand the most incredible thing happened. From my shoulder along my arm and through my hand a current seemed to pass from me to him, while into my heart sprang a love for this stranger that almost overwhelmed me.

And so I discovered that it is not on our forgiving any more than on our goodness that the world's healing hinges, but on His. When He tells us to love our enemies, He gives along with the command, the love itself."[53]

As we attend the temple, study the scriptures, pray more, repent more, and forgive more; we can truly come to know the Lord and His matchless power. Elder Joseph B. Wirthlin counseled, "Drink deeply of living waters. The abundant life is a spiritual life. Too many sit at the banquet table of the gospel of Jesus Christ and merely nibble at the feast placed before them. They go through the motions—attending their meetings, perhaps glancing at their scriptures, repeating family prayers—but their hearts are far away."[54]

As Elder Wirthlin explained, we can get to a point where we are just going through the motions spiritually. We may be going to our church meetings, reading our scriptures, and saying our prayers, but we're not doing so with real meaning or purpose. So if you find your spiritual muscles starting to atrophy—or if you simply feel spiritually apathetic—take the problem to the Lord. Tell him that you desire to drink deeply from the scriptures, and ask Him for the ability and desire to sincerely ponder and pray about them. Ask him to increase your ability to feel the presence of His Spirit, and ask Him to help you learn what He would have you learn in your church meetings.

In a stake conference in January of 2007, then Elder Henry B. Eyring said, "Heavenly Father is your Father, and you were once with Him. It will surprise you when you see Him—How much you know His face and…how much He knows you. God is greater than you can ever imagine."⁵⁵ I know that this is true—that we did know our Heavenly Father in the pre-existence and that He knows us. And I know that part of this life's experience is to learn to know Him again. If you feel far from Heavenly Father, express your love to Him today and ask him to remind you how much He loves you. If you do this in humility, I promise that He will not let you down.

Forgiveness, peace, and true happiness are possible only through the Atonement of Jesus Christ, our Savior and Redeemer. President Thomas S. Monson said, "Through tears and trials, through fears and sorrows, through heartache and loneliness of losing loved ones, there is assurance that life is everlasting. Our Lord and Savior is the living witness that such is so. With all my heart and the fervency of my soul, I lift up my voice in testimony as a special witness and declare that God does live. Jesus is His Son, the Only Begotten of the Father in the flesh. He is our Redeemer; He is our Mediator with the Father. He it was who died on the cross to atone for our sins. He became the first fruits of the Resurrection. Because He died, all shall live again. "Oh, sweet the joy this sentence gives: 'I know that my Redeemer lives!'"⁵⁶

In Exodus 6:7, we read, "And I will take you to me for a people, and I will be to you a God and ye shall know that I am the Lord your God, which bringeth you out from under the burdens of the Egyptians." Early on, the Lord told the Israelites that He would take them out from under their burdens, yet we read that right before the miraculous parting of the Red Sea, the people had no hope and little faith, complaining that they would have been better off staying in Egypt as slaves.

TRUST IN THE LORD

Let's consider this for a moment. Is it sometimes easier to hold onto a burden we have been carrying around for a long time because it's what we know, because it's what we're comfortable and familiar with? Letting go of our burdens and completely giving them to the Lord is our privilege, and it should be our goal. Think about where you are in your life—whether you are holding onto a burden because it's easier than seeing what's on the other side of that sea, or if you are actually trusting in the Lord. You can learn to trust in His timing. You don't need to carry scuba gear around, for it is simply extra weight that you don't need. "And Moses said unto the people, Fear ye not, stand still, and see the salvation of the Lord, which he will shew to you to day: for the Egyptians whom ye have seen to day, ye shall see them again no more for ever. The Lord shall fight for you, and ye shall hold your peace" (Exodus 14:13-14).

There it is! If we don't fear, and if we stand still, the Lord will show us His power in our lives. Let's start today by making a conscious choice to trust in Him, because it certainly is a choice to trust. We must learn for ourselves that He lives, that He loves us, that He truly wants the best for us—and that He will help us fulfill the measure of our creations. Put your scuba gear down and know that He will part your Red Seas. Go forward with faith, and it will surprise you what is on the other side.

NOTES

1. Neal A. Maxwell, "Remember How Merciful the Lord Hath Been," *Ensign*, May 2004, 46
2. Henry B. Eyring, "O Remember, Remember," *Ensign*, November 2007, 67
3. Richard G. Scott, Finding Peace, Happiness and Joy, Salt Lake City: Deseret Book Co., 2007, 109
4. Gordon B. Hinckley, Stand a Little Taller, Salt Lake City: Eagle Gate Publishers, 2001, 13
5. Dallin H. Oaks, "Good, Better, Best," *Ensign*, November 2007, 105
6. Victor Frankl, Man's Search for Meaning, New York: Washington Park Press, 1984, 86–87
7. Ibid
8. Corrie ten Boom with Elizabeth Sherril and John Sherril, The Hiding Place, Old Tappan, NJ: Fleming H. Revell Co., 1971, 198–99
9. Ibid
10. Henry B. Eyring, To Draw Closer to God: A Collection of Discourses, Salt Lake City: Deseret Book Co., 2004, 35
11. "Choose the Right," The Church of Jesus Christ of Latter-Day Saints, Hymn No. 239
12. Boyd K. Packer, "The Candle of the Lord," *Ensign*, January 1983, 53

13. Wendy Watson Nelson, "For Such a Time as This," BYU Women's Conference, May 3, 2007
14. Henry B. Eyring, Union Fort Stake Conference, January 2007, Midvale, Utah
15. David A. Bednar, "In the Strength of the Lord," BYU Idaho Devotional, October 23, 2001
16. Richard G. Scott, "Using the Supernal Gift of Prayer," *Ensign*, May 2007, 8
17. Lucy Mack Smith, History of Joseph Smith, by His Mother, American Fork, UT: Covenant Communications, Inc., 2000, 229
18. Joseph Smith—History 1:14
19. Jeffrey R. and Patricia T. Holland, On Earth As It Is in Heaven, Salt Lake City: Deseret Book Co., 1989, 37–38
20. Neal A. Maxwell, The Neal A. Maxwell Quote Book, ed. Corey H. Maxwell, Salt Lake City: Bookcraft, 2001, 166
21. Boyd K. Packer, Teach Ye Diligently, Salt Lake City: Deseret Book, 1975, 212
22. Gordon B. Hinckley, Way to Be! 9 Ways to Be Happy and Make Something of Your Life, New York: Simon and Schuster, 2002, 18
23. M. Russell Ballard, "The Atonement and the Value of One Soul," *Ensign*, May 2004, 84
24. Gordon B. Hinckley, Way to Be! 9 Ways to Be Happy and Make Something of Your Life, New York: Simon and Schuster, 2002, 18
25. Jeffrey R. and Patricia T. Holland, On Earth As It Is in Heaven, Salt Lake City: Deseret Book Co., 1989, 170

26. Michelle A. Krowl, Women of the Civil War, Petaluma, CA: Pomegranate Communications, Inc., 2006, 42
27. George Albert Smith, The Teachings of George Albert Smith, ed. Robert and Susan McIntosh, Salt Lake City: Bookcraft, 1996, 166–67
28. Abraham Lincoln, Abraham Lincoln's Book of Wit and Wisdom, comp. Louise Bachelder, White Plains, NY: Peter Pauper Press, Inc., 1998
29. "President Thomas S. Monson: On the Lord's Errand," www.lds.org, February 2008
30. Ibid
31. Wives and Daughters of the First Presidency: Excerpts from the 1999 and 1996 BYU Women's Conferences (video), Brigham Young University, 1999
32. Ibid
33. Ibid
34. Ibid
35. Lucy Mack Smith, History of Joseph Smith, by His Mother, American Fork, UT: Covenant Communications, Inc., 2000, 229
36. Ibid
37. M. Russell Ballard, "The Family of the Prophet Joseph Smith," *Ensign*, November 1991, 6
38. Marion D. Hanks, Preparation for Prayer, Salt Lake City: Deseret Book, 1977, 26
39. Margaret D. Nadauld, "The Joy of Womanhood," *Ensign*, November 2000, 14
40. Neal A. Maxwell, "Willing to Submit," *Ensign*, May 1985, 72

41. Dieter F. Uchdorf, "See the End from the Beginning," *Ensign*, May 2006, 43
42. Neal A. Maxwell, The Neal A. Maxwell Quote Book, ed. Corey H. Maxwell, Salt Lake City: Bookcraft, 2001, 339
43. Church News, 24 January 1976, 4
44. Russell M. Nelson, "A Testimony of the Book of Mormon" *Ensign*, November 1999, 71
45. Dallin H. Oaks, "Scripture Reading and Revelation," *Ensign*, January 1995, 8
46. David A. Bednar, "That We May Always Have His Spirit to Be with Us," *Ensign*, May 2006, 30
47. Teachings of the Presidents of the Church: Joseph Smith (Melchizedek Priesthood and Relief Society course of study, 2008–2009). P.132 or (Discourse given by Joseph Smith about July 1839 in Commerce, Illinois;) reported by Willard Richards, in Willard Richards, Pocket Companion pp. 75, 78-79 1st part of quote; 2nd part of quote Letter from Joseph Smith to Isaac Galland, Mar. 22, 1839, Liberty Jail, Liberty, Missouri, published in Times and Seasons, Feb 1840 p.54
48. George Albert Smith, The Teachings of George Albert Smith, ed. Robert and Susan McIntosh, Salt Lake City: Bookcraft, 1996, 86
49. "Where Can I Turn for Peace?" The Church of Jesus Christ of Latter-Day Saints, Hymn No. 129
50. See Jonathan Aitken, John Newton: From Disgrace to Amazing Grace, Wheaton, IL: Crossway Books Publishing, 2007, Quoted in Documentary How Sweet the Sound: The Story of Amazing Grace, by William Christie.

51. Al Rogers, "Amazing Grace: The Story of John Newton," www.reformedreader.org. Originally published in Away Here in Texas, July–August 1996
52. Jeffrey R. Holland, "I Stand All Amazed," *Ensign*, August 1986
53. Corrie ten Boom with Elizabeth Sherril and John Sherril, The Hiding Place, Old Tappan, NJ: Fleming H. Revell Co., 1971, 238
54. Joseph B. Wirthlin, "The Abundant Life," *Ensign*, May 2006, 100
55. Personal notes, Midvale, Utah, Union Fort Stake Conference, January 2007
56. Thomas S. Monson, "I Know That My Redeemer Lives!" *Ensign*, May 2007, 25

ABOUT THE AUTHOR

Michelle L. Martin was raised in Portland, Oregon. She joined the Church of Jesus Christ of Latter-Day Saints at the age of seventeen. Later, Michelle served an LDS mission in the Illinois Peoria Mission. Michelle received a Bachelor's Degree in Dental Hygiene from Weber State University, and a Master's Degree in Public Health from the University of Utah. Currently, Michelle works at the Utah Department of Health as the Oral Health Specialist for the state of Utah. She works with and cares for under-served populations and helps them get access to dental care. She also is the Co-Dental Director for the Utah Special Olympics dental screenings. One of Michelle's loves in life has been traveling abroad on humanitarian trips to provide oral hygiene and dental care. She has been to the Marshall Islands, Vietnam, Peru, Guatemala, and Honduras.

www.ingramcontent.com/pod-product-compliance
Lightning Source LLC
Chambersburg PA
CBHW030527080526
44586CB00011B/354